Teaching Musical Appreciation

Teaching
Musical Appreciation

TERENCE DWYER

LONDON
OXFORD UNIVERSITY PRESS
NEW YORK · TORONTO
1967

Oxford University Press, Ely House, London W.1

GLASGOW NEW YORK TORONTO MELBOURNE WELLINGTON
CAPE TOWN SALISBURY IBADAN NAIROBI LUSAKA ADDIS ABABA
BOMBAY CALCUTTA MADRAS KARACHI LAHORE DACCA
KUALA LUMPUR HONG KONG TOKYO

Printed in Great Britain by
W. & J. Mackay & Co. Ltd., Chatham, Kent

Preface

This book will, I hope, prove useful to all teachers of Musical Appreciation, whether they are concerned with teaching young children, older children, or adults. One does not, of course, approach the problem of teaching these different groups in quite the same way—but the teacher will not need to be told this. What he may not realise is that the fundamentals of the subject are the same for all. Methods of presentation will vary, but the basic objective is the same—to secure, in the pupil, a true appreciation of the music; or rather, as true an appreciation as he can be expected to achieve at his present stage. What this appreciation involves will be revealed by the following chapters.

Few, if any, of the teaching methods expounded in the main part of the book are new or in any sense invented by me. I am indebted for most of them to such writers as Percy A. Scholes, Stewart Macpherson, and Donald Tovey, directly or indirectly. My own contribution lies mainly in the matter of emphasis and advice on the expediency of certain approaches, together with the overall effect of my particular attitude to the teaching of this subject—an attitude which will be abundantly clear to the attentive reader by the end of the book.

I have included a final chapter on the philosophy of listening to music. Whilst this may not seem essential to a

book which is for the most part severely practical, I believe that every teacher of music should have a carefully-thought-out attitude to the whole process of listening; in fact, should be convinced of the true *raison d'être* of his art. Some readers may care to read Chapter 8 following Chapter 1, as there is a kind of direct link between them; nevertheless the book is best read in correct sequence, because the final chapter sums up and explains (by implication) the reasons for the various practical procedures suggested in the main part of the book. That this final chapter offers unprovable explanations in certain controversial fields, I am well aware; all that I ask of the reader who cannot agree with me is that he should carefully form and hold to a philosophy of his own which shall be devotedly carried out daily in his own teaching.

Finally, I would like to express my grateful thanks to the following friends and colleagues who have helped me by reading all or part of the script and by making various suggestions for improving it: Mr. A. L. Chattaway, Mr. C. J. Newby, and Mr. L. R. Rogers.

T.D.

Contents

1. What is the Task?

Few people nowadays question the validity of the teaching of Musical Appreciation in schools and other places of learning. Its value has become accepted: indeed, where it is not to be found it is usually sought after eagerly. Some music teachers wish they dare attempt it; most music teachers do attempt it. Of the latter but a small proportion can feel that they are unable to improve their methods. A great deal of diffidence surrounds the efforts of even the best teachers—one might say, of *especially* the best teachers. Diffidence, indeed, could be said to be the true distinguishing feature of Musical Appreciation teaching. But the teacher should be diffident about the right thing. If he is diffident about his musical knowledge—of technical devices such as fugue and sonata form—of different musical instruments and how they work—of standard compositions and facts of musical history—in short, about his basic equipment as a music teacher, there is no justifiable reason why this diffidence should be allowed to continue. Let him repair his deficiencies as soon as possible. Let him go to the many excellent textbooks that exist for this purpose. He is mature and musical and can quickly profit by the written word, unlike most of his pupils, who will need guidance and clear illustration in order to understand music. And I should emphasise that this applies, with some modification, to the non-specialist teacher in the junior school. Even one who is unable to play a note, but is fond of music, should be able to teach himself enough facts from books, and by careful listening to suitable examples, to teach what is necessary in a junior school. Of course, our teacher need not postpone his teaching of Musical Appreciation until *all* his deficiencies are repaired and every gap in his knowledge made good. He should teach (with diffidence!) what he can in the meanwhile. As Percy Scholes pointed out, No Teaching is as much a crime against youth as Bad Teaching. But the teacher should make speedy efforts to remove this unjustifiable cause of his diffidence. What, then, *is* justifiable cause?

To answer this, I must first digress and examine the nature of music and of the listener's response to it. Music is a language. It conveys ideas, emotions, and attitudes (like all the arts) through a kind of code. The composer has ideas to express, he encodes them into musical sounds, we decode them and understand the ideas. The composer has communicated with us; music was his medium. He might have chosen any other medium—painting, had he been an artist; dancing, if he had known how; words, if he could have found adequate ones; gestures, if he were a mime. But his gifts lay in a particular direction, so he used music as being his best form of communication. Note that, even in those cases where a composer may have composed to please himself and not to communicate with an audience, the general theory still holds good: the music is the expression of his ideas, and if it gets to an audience who can understand it the communication is made whether intended or not. (Don't be distracted here by the presence of the *performer*. He is a necessary part of the medium—the messenger boy or the telegraph wire through which the message must flow. He is no part of the creative process;

or if he is, then to that extent he becomes a composer and shares in the expression of ideas.)

It is apparent that if this language is to work properly we receivers must understand it. This is where the trouble starts. We do not all respond similarly to the same piece of music. One may find a piece solemn, another peaceful, another tragic, another joyous. (These descriptions have all been applied, for example, to the middle theme of Holst's *Jupiter*.) And here a fallacious attitude often manifests itself. 'We are all different,' say some, 'we have different temperaments and different upbringings. We are bound to respond to music differently. Let each man find what he can and will in music. He has a perfect right to his opinion. The world would be a dull place if we all thought the same.' With the second part of this statement I cannot agree. We are bound to respond to music differently, yes. This is inevitable. *But it is not desirable.* We ought to try to respond to music similarly in so far as this is possible. To the best of my knowledge no one has ever suggested that it would be desirable for everyday verbal language to be interpreted according to the temperament and experience of each individual. In point of fact, such differences do arise. (I have spent fruitless hours arguing with friends and colleagues only to find that we didn't differ at all in our views, but had foundered over the question of different interpretations of some common word. And Mendelssohn said, '. . . words seem to me to be so ambiguous, so vague, and so easily misunderstood in comparison with genuine music.') But we all agree, I think, that such differences constitute an undesirable barrier to communication through the medium of words. It seems to me high time this line of reasoning was applied to music. It might well be true that we should all enjoy music far more if we *did* all think the same. The process of communication from creator to listener would be more complete and unambiguous. But can it be achieved? What conditions would be necessary to achieve it?

When a piece of music is composed it is because the composer feels a certain way and expresses himself in sound. Why does he feel this way? It is because of his inborn temperament, plus his total life experiences, that he feels just the way he does. Why does he express himself a particular way in sound? It is because his knowledge of musical technique and tradition suggests (perhaps subconsciously) certain procedures and so he adopts them. How are we to understand him perfectly? The only way, presumably, would be to have an exactly similar temperament to his, to have had an exactly similar total of life experiences, and to have gained precisely the same knowledge of music. This is obviously very difficult! And even if we could do it with one composer, we would clearly be excluded from understanding other composers. The situation seems impossible.

Fortunately we are saved by two all-important facts. First, that a good many emotions and life attitudes are common to all men, and many others can be sympathetically understood even if they have not actually been experienced (e.g. murderous rage or despairing love). Second, that composers have tended to use a common language, i.e. they influence each other; they do not each invent a fresh musical language (or if they do, as with some modern composers, they risk paying the price of non-comprehension by others). True, this common language has altered gradually during the course of history. This means, for example, that the language of Purcell's time is not that of Tchaikovsky's. But we have no more trouble understanding both than we do of understanding, say, Shakespeare and T. S. Eliot.

And so it would seem from my argument that there is a definite, once-and-for-all meaning to every piece of music, if only we can find it. 'Meaning' (like all other words!) is ambiguous, of course. By using it I intend to convey 'a true reliving by us of the composer's ideas, feelings, and attitudes, in so far as we are capable of this'. How do we reach this meaning? First, by experiencing everyday emotions and other basic life situations such as are likely to find expression in music (which is why younger people are more likely to err in their understanding), and second, by hearing much music of all kinds, in other words familiarising ourselves with the language in all its dialects and period mannerisms (which is why less musically experienced people are more likely to err in their understanding). To put it very simply, to understand music you have to live life as fully and as long as possible, and you have to listen to lots and lots of music!

I hope the reason for my long digression will now become clear. To sum up:

(1) We don't all interpret music alike.
(2) But we ought to try.
(3) This involves having much musical experience.
(4) Failing this, who will guide us?

The answer to the last question is: the most musically experienced person we can find. And in your school this means *you*! You must guide your pupils, for you have had more musical experience than they have. And now you see what there really is to be diffident about. Because you are a modest person and the thought of this responsibility

appals you. 'Am I,' you may ask, 'to impose my interpretations on the pupils? I don't feel qualified.' Well,
you're the best man around, so it's up to you to try. But
please, *please*, never stop trying to widen your taste and
knowledge, or for that matter your sympathy for your
pupils' *lack* of taste and knowledge. To put the matter
clearly, this kind of diffidence is a priceless asset: woe to
the teacher who loses it! Secure in his infallibility, he will
tend to lose patience with pupils who do not see things his
way. He will gradually become blind to the existence of
the difficulties facing those whose experience does not
equal his own. This diffidence, then, we all ought to feel,
but have to put aside (in a sense) in order to do our job.
So we take confidence *from the very existence of the diffidence*
and proceed with what may be called 'diffident confidence'.
But let's go back to the phrase 'impose my interpretations'.
I'm not sure we want that exactly. 'Impose' is a loaded
word, full of implications of duress and dogmatism. This
would be a poor way to encourage love of music. You must
teach your interpretations, but in a subtle way. Better than
'No, Jones, it's *not* a funny piece. Can't you see it's very
tragic?' would be, 'Yes, it can seem funny at first. But see
if you think so after a few hearings. I believe it's quite
serious, really.' Better still is not to make too much point
about the 'meaning' anyway, but to teach such facts about
the piece as will enable it to be understood in the proper
light. An example will make this clearer. It would be futile
with Bach's Brandenburg Concerto No. 3 to say, 'This is
very colourful music. Do you hear how one instrument is
followed by another of a different kind? These dramatic
changes allow the imagination to create the images of
adventures and battles'; or of the second movement of
Rimsky-Korsakov's *Scheherazade*, 'Grasp the first theme

above all. Everything else follows logically from it. You must listen to the middle and the bass as well as the treble. Often the main theme is buried underneath, with other tunes running above it. Then the themes will change places without warning. Keep alert and follow the simultaneous lines of melody.' But exchange the two remarks and we make more sense. We have to teach such facts, or to suggest such approaches, as we know to be suitable to the piece in hand and to the pupils concerned. In other words, the secret of teaching Musical Appreciation is to know just what to say about a given piece, to a given class, at a given time. There is an old story about a boiler system that went wrong. The owner of the house could not get it to function, and eventually sent for a heating engineer. The latter made a careful inspection, then drew out a hammer and struck one blow at a certain spot on the boiler. Immediately the system functioned perfectly and the engineer departed. When the householder received a bill for £10 he thought this a bit steep and demanded a more detailed account. He received the following:

For hitting boiler with hammer	1d.
For knowing where to hit	£9 19s. 11d.
	£10 0s. 0d.

We must know where to hit. Sometimes in our lessons we need say only a very few words, but they must be the right words. Sometimes a long preparation is necessary, with the introduction of technical terms. *No one method can always succeed.* By our study of many composers and many methods of teaching, and by our study of our pupils, we shall know *which* pieces to play, *when* to play them, and *what* to say about them. Let's look at that in more detail.

Choose your piece of music according to your knowledge of:

(1) The pupil. He has to be capable of understanding and enjoying the piece, in the light of his temperament and previous knowledge.

(2) You. You have to be capable of presenting the piece with genuine enthusiasm. Pupils will always detect hypocrisy sooner or later. (If you have a blind spot for a particular composer or piece, this creates a problem. We will take this up in a later chapter.)

(3) The general picture of the child's education in Musical Appreciation. What has been left undone? Are we showing too much bias towards a certain kind of music, or are we giving our pupils a broad, inclusive picture?

(4) Topicality. The alert teacher will use any interest already aroused by other means. Is there a concert on this week in the local hall? Is it Easter soon? Is it Bach's tercentenary? Has one of the class just bought a flute? Did we have a song by this composer in the singing lesson this week?

Choose what you say about the piece of music according to:

(1) The piece itself. Is it contrapuntal? Does it depend upon key changes? Is it rhythmically interesting?—and so on.

(2) The pupil. Will what you say be understood by all, or most, of the class?

(3) You. Say only what you can say with personal conviction and authority. Getting opinions and facts secondhand from textbooks is useless unless you can understand them thoroughly and agree with them thoroughly.

(4) The mood everyone's in. We're all alert? Off we go into a detailed analysis. It's that end-of-term feeling? Let's

just relax and listen. We want to encourage a love of music, not kill it.

(5) Previous knowledge. The same piece of music will have different approaches with classes of different previous experience, even when all the foregoing factors are the same. In fact, the same piece might well be presented to the *same* class at several stages in their education, with a different approach each time.

The matter doesn't end, of course, with what the teacher says. When does he say it—before, during, or after the music? And how many times does he play the piece? Does the teacher show any pictures? What do the pupils do? Do they speak, or write? If so, what? A few moments ago I said, 'No one method can always succeed', and this is important. The teacher must have many methods, many lines of approach at his finger-tips; not only different ways of looking at music but different methods of classroom presentation and different ways of involving the pupils. And this brings me to my next important point. The pupil must be involved. Indeed, unless he is involved, more or less deeply, in every Musical Appreciation lesson, then that lesson has failed. However good the material and presentation of a lesson, if it falls on deaf ears it goes for nothing. One of the best speakers on music I know is Antony Hopkins. However, his interesting and illuminating talks, as broadcast over the radio, would be wasted if loudspeakers were to broadcast his talks to empty classrooms all over the country, or if no one were to switch on at all. Indeed, I sometimes feel sorry for Antony Hopkins that he does not experience that two-way communication between teacher and pupil which goes on in the classroom. He cannot know (at least, at the time) that his points are going home to the listener. And in this respect the class teacher, however poor,

has the advantage over the expert broadcaster: he is alive
and on the spot, he is in communication with individual
pupils, and can secure and evaluate some sort of response
from them. The class teacher, then, must know what the
progress of his pupils is. He can talk to them and test them,
discuss with them. He does not have to talk *at* them.

Now let's recapitulate in brief:

(1) Music is a communicative process from composer to
listener. Its meaning is understood properly only by those
with a wide knowledge of music.

(2) The task of the teacher is twofold: (*a*) to guide those
with less musical knowledge than himself, (*b*) constantly to
increase his own musical knowledge.

(3) The teacher brings about this guidance by knowing
how to say, or do, the right thing at the right time. This is
his professional skill—it's what he is entitled to charge
£9. 19*s*. 11*d*. for.

(4) The pupil's reaction is important, and it is the
teacher's job to watch it and nurture it.

I am well aware that some of the more experienced of
my readers may find much to quarrel with in my line of
reasoning. For instance, they may wish to argue that music
is other things besides a language, that it does *not* convey
one definite meaning, and that very experienced musicians
differ in their interpretations of a piece, that the teacher
should confine himself to facts and refrain from offering
an interpretation. Well, I don't care. I believe that the
teacher's most priceless asset is *infectious enthusiasm*, without
which all his other skills will count for very little. Being
afraid to offer a point of view may be safe, but it probably
won't stimulate anyone to love a piece of music. Let the
teacher reveal his views, right or wrong. He may have
based them on ignorance or misconceptions; his views may

be distorted, ludicrous even. He may well change them
next year. (He *will*, because he is constantly seeking to
improve his taste.) At least he believes in them and his
pupils will sense this. Once the love of music has been
passed on the rest can follow. Of course, if the teacher has
no definite views about the meaning of a piece he can
presumably do little harm anyway!

In the following chapters various approaches to the
subject will be discussed. Before proceeding it will be well
to make a few further points:

(1) Although there are many ways of leading people to
love music, and none need be despised, nevertheless some
are likely to be more valuable than others, depending
on the age and experience of the listener.

(2) No one on earth can understand a piece properly by
hearing it only once. All teaching schemes should involve
repeated hearings.

(3) Wherever possible (and that's nearly always) the
pupil should be given something to listen *for*.

All right! Now, keeping our diffidence (caused by the
unavoidable responsibility we have of helping to mould
other people's musical taste), we begin to shoulder the
task. In fact, to stress the importance of enthusiasm as the
main force in doing so, I would urge the young and inexperienced teacher to read no further for the time being.
Put this book down, go into your classroom and take a
favourite record or piano piece. Try showing your class just
what it is that makes you fond of it. Never mind about
being clever; try to communicate your love of music. Go
on, do it!

Well, did it work? No? Why? I see, they didn't all like
it. Well, really, that's expecting a lot. Didn't *anyone* like it?

Two or three. All right: *you have succeeded*. Your efforts weren't entirely wasted. Between five and ten per cent of the class is a good start. What you have to do in future lessons is to increase that percentage. I hope the following pages will be a little help in lightening the load.

2. Teaching Colour

The visual arts have borrowed musical terms such as rhythm, harmony, and counterpoint. We have retaliated by taking words such as form, colour, dark, light, etc. By 'colour' we mean any of the following:

(1) Timbre or tone: that is the *quality* of musical sound, as distinct from pitch, duration, and volume (*tone colour*).
(2) The effect given by harmony (*harmonic colour*).
(3) The effect given by registers, high or low (*light or dark colour*).
(4) The effect given by volume contrasts or accents (*dramatic colour*).

(This last is a rather loose use of the term, but we *do* speak about 'So-and-so's colourful interpretation', where we really refer to volume contrasts, perhaps also to *rubato*.)

Of all these meanings the first is the most important and the most usual. By the use of different voices or instruments a composer makes his colour effects and his colour contrasts. Suppose only one instrument existed, e.g. the piano, then this meaning could hardly apply, as the composer could not change his tone colours (except to a very limited extent) and thus oppose them to one another. But other instruments do exist, and this variety of resource is used, broadly speaking, in two ways: (1) by the choice of certain voices or instruments for use throughout a piece, the composer suffuses his piece with a particular colour, (2) by changing from one instrument or group of instruments to another, or from voice to instrument, perhaps in a kaleidoscopic fashion, the composer gains the effect of colour contrast. Examples of the first method are: (a) Bach's aria 'For love my Saviour now is dying' from the St. Matthew Passion, for soprano with flute and two oboi da caccia; (b) Sibelius's *Swan of Tuonela*, dominated by cor anglais; (c) Britten's *Serenade*, for tenor, horn, and strings, a combination suited to the romantic, nocturnal poems involved. Examples of the second method are: (a) second movement of Beethoven's Symphony No. 7 in A, where each main section of the music has its particular instrumental colouring, especially the kaleidoscopic Coda; (b) most of Tchaikovsky's orchestral music (though it is true that the shorter pieces such as those in the *Nutcracker* Suite tend to fall into the first category above); (c) second movement, Play of the Couples, from Bartók's Concerto for Orchestra, where pairs of wind instruments succeed each other. It should not be thought that colour contrasts belong exclusively to music since 1750. Look at, for example, John Bull's *The King's Hunting Jigge*, where passages are frequently repeated in a different octave. This music was written for the virginals, an instrument which changes its tone appreciably from high to low. The contrast of register thus has more point than it would have on a piano. Look also at John Wilbye's 'Sweet Honey-sucking Bees', a madrigal for five voices in which there are several passages for the upper three voices, echoed by the lower three voices (middle part doing double duty), giving, like the Bull example, a tone-colour contrast as well as a register contrast. (Mozart used exactly the same device at the beginning of his String Quintet in G minor). However, it remains true that music before 1750 on the whole ignores colour as a potent factor in musical expression and we must normally look to later music for the clearest examples of it.

Now of all the approaches to Musical Appreciation which can be conveniently taught in the classroom, the colour approach is one of the simplest, both to teach and to learn. It can be taught at any stage, but is particularly suitable as a starting-point for younger children. By 'colour approach' I mean the tone-colour aspect, of course; not the others mentioned at the beginning of the chapter. But I shall include in it a consideration of the *performer* and his contribution. This may seem illogical but it's not really. When we consider tone colour, we are thinking of the *kind* of sounds made, rather than the nature of the musical logic involved in the other factors of melody, rhythm, texture, harmony, form, and style. We think of what does the performing, rather than what is performed. Our attention is, for the time being, on the player and his instrument (or voice) and not on the composer. And so it is that the young child (and the less intellectual side of the adult) is interested in musicians rather than in music. We can make use of this interest and pave the way for other approaches to music by developing it systematically. That this interest in performers is widespread in immature minds is attested by the attitude of young people towards their 'pop' idols. The interest in the music is present, of course, but often it is secondary to an admiration of the performers involved. Even when young people are *trying* to listen to great music, the things which stick in their minds are often the dramatic uses of instruments—the *fortissimo* drum roll, the trombone chords, the clarinet cadenza, and so on. I remember at the age of 15 being taken to one of the excellent Robert Mayer orchestral concerts for schoolchildren and hearing Dvořák's 'New World' Symphony for the first time. Alas for all the subtleties of the music! The only impressions I carried away with me were of banging drums, whirling bows, and loud brass chords. But the seeds were sown. Perhaps I had to get such things out of my system before I could really get down to listening. In one way I was ready to listen to great music: I could play the violin and piano after a fashion, and I was a good singer in the local church choir. But this wasn't enough. In those days we were taught nothing at all about music at grammar school—it wasn't on the curriculum. Had I been thoroughly grounded in the instruments of the orchestra at school, and maybe in some elementary facts of musical form, I could have got more benefit from the music. But I took from that performance what I was ready for. For days I admired the conductor and the players (though I've forgotten now who they were!) and imagined myself going through the actions I had seen.

By beginning with the performer and his instrument, the teacher will make use of human interest. Let him not stay there, however. He should proceed gently but inevitably towards the music itself. It is not always realised, for example, what junior-school pupils are capable of understanding about music. This kind of work is the very least that they should attempt. As soon as it is absorbed there are other matters to occupy their attention: see Chapter 6 for suggestions.

As early as possible, then, children should be brought into contact with as many instruments and performers as possible:

(1) *Within the school*. The teacher will play the piano, presumably, but should bring any other instruments he possesses to show the children, even if he plays them badly.

The pupils will not mind this, provided the teacher doesn't pretend anything. I knew a science teacher once who possessed a massive bass recorder. He could only play one musical phrase on it, but children to whom he showed it were invariably interested. So bring that guitar to school—or even that mouth-organ! And pester your colleagues—they may have hidden talents. Of course, encourage whatever instrumental tuition is possible in your school, taking full advantage of any facilities extended by the local authority for the provision of visiting instrumental teachers. Make the pupils who do learn an instrument feel proud of this. Give the other pupils opportunities to see and hear them at work.

(2) *Outside the school.* Arrange visits to local concerts, operas, etc. But be sure that the children aren't bored by having too much to take in. Sometimes it is possible for visiting performers to give a recital within the school, for a reasonable fee. Try to persuade your head teacher to let them come, even if your requisition has to suffer. The interest aroused by the visit will last for weeks, or even years.

(3) *On television, films, radio and gramophone.* Try to interest the children in a few famous performers. It does not matter how few, or even that you have not chosen the best, but that some star performers are noticed and admired. Let the pop singers have a few rivals!

At some stage, then, in the life of a child he will have acquired a mass of information about various performers and instruments. It is time to organise this knowledge and to add to it. Here are some possible schemes.

(1) How instruments work.
(2) Some famous performers.
(3) Solos for various instruments and voices.
(4) Instruments of the world.

(5) The instruments of the orchestra.
(6) Colour at work in music.
(7) Various musical media.
(8) Score reading.

And there should be others. If the reader can think of one or two for himself, he is probably well on the road to being a good teacher of Musical Appreciation. Let us look at the above schemes in more detail.

(1) *How instruments work*

It is best to start with simple instruments such as drums and bugles. Pupils should be shown that all instruments normally consist of three parts: a vibrator, a resonator, and a pitch control. (Discretion is used whether to employ these words!) Then we move through more complicated instruments such as trumpet, trombone, xylophone, harp, to the most complicated: violin, clarinet, piano, etc. The classification of strings, wind, and percussion is established, but we don't bother at this stage with the subdivision into brass and woodwind, or keep the harp and other plucked instruments out of the 'strings' family, unless these questions arise naturally. The class must *see and hear* the instruments (preferably the real thing; failing that, pictures and records) and be shown just how they work. Don't overlook the humble classroom piano, and try to take the pupils to visit a local organ and show them (or get the organist to show them) its various resources and how it all works.

With older pupils more detail can be given. Simple acoustics are not out of place: how the air vibrates, the principle of shortening a string or air column to get higher notes, and so on. With a practically minded class there is much to be said for a project involving the making of the pupils' own instruments—various percussion instruments, bamboo pipes, even guitars have been made. (A public schoolboy once made his own two-manual harpsichord!) The interest thus aroused is enormous and can be turned to good account.

(2) *Some famous performers*

Try starting with someone well known, whose records are easily available, and do a study of him and his instrument. Then move on to one or two other performers of the same instrument. It all depends who is the man of the moment. Just now it seems that Julian Bream would be a good choice for the guitar, to be followed by Segovia. Then we would move to another instrument, say the piano, and choose a well-known performer such as John Ogdon. So it would go, from instrument to instrument, till the children had built up a gallery of famous performers. Pupils would be encouraged to bring newspaper and magazine cuttings (though the teacher will probably have to do most of this) and to follow the careers of the chosen musicians. Singers and conductors could be brought in also. After a spell of this, perhaps some performers of the not-too-distant past might be studied, such as Kreisler, Caruso, and Paderewski (it all depends what records are available!), or even of the more remote past, such as Paganini and Liszt. Modern recordings would have to be used, of course, to show the *kind* of performance they gave, but contemporary accounts of these players could make interesting reading for a short time.

(3) *Solos for various instruments and voices*

The idea here is to build up a listener's repertoire of pieces showing different instruments and voices used in solos. It is inevitable that to some extent this method will combine itself with one or both of the previous methods; however, the emphasis is slightly different—here we think more of the sound of the music than of the instrument (as a piece of mechanism) or of the player (as a person). We are interesting ourselves more truly in the colours of music. We take one colour at a time: for example, a lesson on violin solos will have perhaps three or four short pieces played. Similarly a lesson on the oboe and one on the flute may follow. Remembering the value of repeated hearings, a lesson should follow in which the best piece of each of the previous three lessons is played, for revision and comparison purposes. Perhaps the pupils could even hear the second movement of Bach's Brandenburg Concerto No. 2, in which these three instruments all play together. (But take care: we may not be ready for the problems created by the existence of counterpoint, so we would keep off that aspect and concentrate on the colours.) And so it goes on, through the instruments and main types of voice. Eventually the pupils should be able to think automatically of at least one famous and significant solo for any important instrument you can name. And don't forget organ, guitar, harp, and other slightly less familiar instruments. You might even feel inclined to play a Milt Jackson record to show the vibraphone, for example, or Charlie Parker for the saxophone.

(4) *Instruments of the world*

You would have to do a bit of special research for this. I think probably you'd have to be a special sort of person, too! Maybe you've actually been to India and have brought back a *vina*. Or have a very special collection of records. Or have the gift of making pictures come alive by your verbal and imaginative powers. Or maybe you teach geography, too, and want to link it with music. I don't think *I* could use this approach—certainly I've never tried it. Why mention it, then? Because I believe in variety of approach, and especially I believe that the teacher should use whatever approach suits *him*. Don't feel obliged to follow the beaten track all the time. So, if this idea appeals to you and you think you can tackle it, go ahead. I make you a present of the idea, but I can't help you to carry it out! Beware, however, that the class doesn't get stuffed full with a lot of information which will be largely useless to them. Time available for teaching this subject is usually limited, and it is more important to teach about instruments which the pupils will actually come across. However, this course should work if it is short, interesting, and is used to follow up an existing knowledge of the more familiar instruments.

(5) *The instruments of the orchestra*

This very useful scheme is so overworked nowadays that to some teachers it seems synonymous with Musical Appreciation. It is, of course, only one of several possible approaches to the study of instruments. Its drawback is that it excludes so many useful and desirable instruments which don't happen to belong to the club. Twenty years ago we used to think that the piano dominated the scene too much: that there was the dangerous equation 'music = piano'. Nowadays, with the spread of radio and gramophone records, the danger is that the orchestra dominates too much. We don't want our pupils to think 'music = orchestra', so if you do use this course, follow it by examples of non-orchestral instruments and non-orchestral music. However, for colour interest the modern orchestra is unbeatable, so we proceed, keeping the above warning in mind.

This approach differs from the others in that we show the internal organisation of the orchestra, how each member contributes to the success of the whole. I always like to precede a course on the orchestra by a few lessons about the human voice, showing first the classification into soprano, alto, tenor, and bass; then showing how a quartet or choir combine to make *harmony*. With this behind us we look at the orchestra and see the three main families of strings, woodwind and brass as three independent 'choirs', with four main instruments in each family, corresponding to S.A.T. and B. The choirs often unite in a 'Three Choirs' Festival' or lend one of their members to another choir, and so on. Of course, I am aware that this is not the whole truth—there are such things as mezzo-sopranos and baritones, piccolos and cors anglais; the violas *don't* take the alto part usually, nor do the wind groups work out with one kind of instrument to each voice; but nothing can be more tedious than telling the whole truth when it is not needed. At an early stage children would only be confused by being told exactly what happens about the distribution of harmony amongst the orchestra (perhaps you're confused yourself?). The best thing is to make things *simple to remember*. If the class know how a four-part choir involves a top melody with three supporting parts, they will see the parallel when it is applied to the orchestra. So even if it misleads them for a time, get them to think on the following lines:

Voice	*Strings*	*Woodwind*	*Brass*
Soprano	Violin	Flute	Trumpet
Alto	Viola	Oboe	Horn
Tenor	Cello	Clarinet	Trombone
Bass	Double Bass	Bassoon	Tuba

Percussion instruments mark the rhythm.

It's not all that far from the truth, anyway, and it's comprehensible. If I thought I could get away with it, I'd throw the percussion in at this stage and make four voices out of that! Then we'd have four families and four instruments in each family, and very neat and tidy, too! But, alas, it won't work, so we are content with the above scheme, until one day we (or rather the pupils) are ready for the whole truth.

As with the previous schemes, each instrument is demonstrated separately and then in families, if possible, before being put into the full orchestra. Several excellent records exist today specially demonstrating the instruments of the orchestra, for example *Instruments of the Orchestra* directed by Menuhin. Britten's *Young Person's Guide to the Orchestra* is a 'must'; better still the film *Instruments of the Orchestra* for which it was written. Prokofiev's *Peter and the Wolf* and Saint-Saëns' *Carnival of the Animals* also clearly demonstrate various instruments. Various wall charts showing pictures of the instruments are available, and are commonly used as permanent decorations on music-room walls. (Don't have *anything* as a permanent decoration, or familiarity will stale its effectiveness.)

(6) *Colour at work in music*

This is the most difficult aspect to teach, but the most worth-while, and is suitable for older children or adults. The idea is to see the composer's use of colour actually at work in a piece of music and to appreciate the effects of his colour changes and combinations. This approach presupposes a knowledge of instruments, or rather the ability to identify instruments by sound (not necessarily the same thing). Choose a record with several clear-cut melodies for one type of instrument, for example the first four

movements of Kodály's *Háry János* Suite. Play the record
and comment during the music:

'Oboe here . . . clarinet . . . violins . . . horns coming in a moment, notice what a sharp contrast it is from
violins . . . oboe again . . .'

This, of course, is in the nature of teaching or revision.
To secure a response from the class, get them to call out
the name of the prominent instrument. You must be prepared for a certain amount of confusion, with people
calling out, teacher correcting them, and so on. In fact,
the music, as music, may well get swamped at times. This
doesn't matter—we're not listening to music at the
moment, we're practising a particular skill which will
prove very useful to us when we *do* listen to music.

The procedure just described is but a step, however, and
of little real value in itself. It is painful to read some of
the essays I am occasionally presented with by young
people aged 15–20. 'First there was a tune on the violins,
then the cellos had a turn, then the oboe. After this a bang
on the kettledrum and then the full orchestra played. A
little while later there was a wind solo, the oboe, I
think . . .' and so it goes on. This in an essay purporting
to be a critical description of the music! It is as if we described a great painting thus: 'In the top left-hand corner
there is a patch of blue, then it gets whiter as you go across.
Lower down there is a bit of red, then a sort of purple . . .'
Of course, neither of these efforts constitutes complete and
accurate description, let alone a criticism of any kind. Nor
can they, since they concern themselves solely with a
cataloguing of the one aspect of colour. However, description and criticism have to begin somewhere, so this
kind of thing is all right so long as it does not become an
end in itself. It is one of the many necessary steps the

listener must take in order to understand music and talk intelligently about it.

The next important step is to think about colour combinations and the reason for them. For example, the class should listen to the 'Viennese Musical Clock' from Kodály's *Háry János* and discover for itself that no stringed instruments are used. It should then try to suggest a reason for this. In both the first and third movements of the same suite there are interesting passages whose effect depends not only on a horn melody but on the special nature of the accompaniment, considered both as a rhythmic figure and as an orchestral colour. An analogy with art can be drawn here: it is like a clear shape drawn in blue, with orange squiggles repeated to make a background. Members of the class should be asked to find other passages of colour combinations which interest them, to name the instruments, and to try to find an equivalent in words (not necessarily in visual terms) to describe the effect gained. *The Young Person's Guide to the Orchestra* should be gone through again, the class noting the *accompaniments* to the various solos and commenting on the choice of instruments. The teacher should select other records which contain, to his mind, passages of skilful orchestration and present them to the class, trying to show them what appeals to him.

Once all this kind of thing has been done, it can always be referred to in passing when the class is engaged in some quite different activity, e.g. a study of form. 'Now we come to the recapitulation. Notice how the first subject is now played by the clarinet instead of the violins. This is a striking use of clarinet colour and is just right after the previous violin passage. Don't let it put you off recognising the tune as the tune of the first subject.'

The last sentence in the above imaginary teacher's remark serves to remind us how strong an impression musical colour makes on many listeners. To them the tone quality is so all-important that they really won't recognise as identical the same tune played on widely different instruments. (I must admit to this fault myself when listening to a piece for the first time.) The reason is that we normally hear a theme as a pitch-rhythm-tempo-colour-volume-harmony *complex*. Change one or more features and we have a new complex. It's difficult enough as it is exercising the memory to recognise themes over the time-lapse of a piece of music. If a composer changes the instrument, that's one more thing to make it harder. So have sympathy for your pupils and give them the right sort of records to help overcome this. These are of two kinds: (1) complete solos by one instrument (say oboe). These enable us to see that one instrument can produce many different themes and we learn to remember them *as themes*; (2) pieces involving immediate repetition of a short theme by one instrument after another. Grieg's 'Morning' from *Peer Gynt* comes to mind, and the fugue from *The Young Person's Guide*. Many development sections from symphonies and overtures (e.g. *Egmont*) should also prove useful here.

(7) *Various musical media*

This means string quartet, oboe quartet, clarinet quintet, wind quintet, violin sonata, organ fugue, piano prelude, overture, ballet music, piano concerto, church cantata, song cycle, lied, opera, etc. etc. What we do is to introduce the pupils to each of these (or as many of them as we can), partly to show them that these are the main channels of expression open by tradition to the composer, also to define each one clearly; and partly to teach the sounds of the various instruments and voices, as colours. In fact, with a bit of care in the selection of our examples, we might manage to combine the above two aims with a skeleton history of music, bringing in the most important composers. Here, for example, is a quick try on my part. By all means improve on it if you wish.

Morley: Madrigal, 'Sing we and chant it'
Purcell: Recit. and aria: 'When I am laid in earth', from the opera *Dido and Aeneas*
Handel: Organ Concerto in B♭
Bach: French Suite No. 5 for harpsichord *or* Orchestral Suite No. 2 for flute and strings (extracts)
Haydn: 'Clock' Symphony, slow movement
Mozart: 'Hunt' Quartet, finale
Beethoven: 'Moonlight' Sonata, 1st movement
Rossini: *Thieving Magpie* Overture *or*
Weber: *Oberon* Overture
Schubert: Lied, 'The Erl King'
Mendelssohn: 'Lift thine eyes', Trio from the oratorio *Elijah*
Chopin: Any piano preludes
Schumann: Piano Concerto, 1st movement *or*
Grieg: ditto
Liszt: Hungarian Rhapsody No. 2, for piano solo
Wagner: Prize Song from *The Mastersingers*
Berlioz: March to the Scaffold, from the *Fantastic Symphony or*
Dvořák: 'New World' Symphony, slow movement
Verdi: Quartet from the opera *Rigoletto*
Franck: Violin Sonata, finale
Tchaikovsky: Excerpts from the ballet *Swan Lake*
Elgar: 'Enigma' Variations, theme and first three variations
Debussy: Sonata for Flute, Viola, and Harp, 1st movement
Sibelius: Tone poem, *The Swan of Tuonela*
Stravinsky: Excerpts from the ballet *Petrushka*

Bartók: Play of the Couples, 2nd movement of Concerto for
   Orchestra
Walton: Excerpt from the oratorio *Belshazzar's Feast*
Arnold: *Three shanties*, for wind quintet
Britten: Sea Interlude 'Storm' from the opera *Peter Grimes*

These twenty-six pieces, treated adequately, could provide anything from a term's to a year's work, depending
on the time available. The pupils could take notes, either
about the instruments, or the type of piece, or the composer: but not all three unless you want them to do more
writing than listening!

(8) *Score reading*

This is an extremely interesting and useful approach to
colour. It is also an approach to other aspects of music and
will be referred to again in its due place. It does, however,
presuppose a certain knowledge of reading music on the
pupils' part; alternatively an intelligent desire to do so. It
is therefore particularly suitable for older pupils or even
untrained adults, but it does call for patience all round,
particularly in the earliest stages when the class is struggling
with the unfamiliar layout of the staves. Don't waste time
and money buying sets of miniature scores for your beginners; get Roger Fiske's *Score Reading, Book 1: Orchestration*
and all your problems will be solved. Under one cover
there are enough pieces for one or two terms' work, and
the emphasis is on colour throughout. Obviously there is a
strong affinity here with method (6) and of course score
reading can be used to back it up, also methods (5) and (7)
if desired.

So I have described eight possible methods of dealing
with the question of 'colour' in music. It is obvious that

some of these will combine well with each other—indeed, it is desirable that they should. Don't be inflexible just because you have embarked upon a particular scheme. Take opportunities in a lesson to refer across, not only to other aspects of colour, but to any other related musical topic which may naturally fit into the lesson. When colour has been introduced and learnt to some extent the pupil is ready for more challenging ways of listening to music.

3. Teaching Texture

Here we come to a matter of prime importance in listening to music. So important it is that I would unhesitatingly pick it out as being the acid test of the good listener. Can he hear, reasonably clearly, what is going on beneath the obvious surface melody? Can he hear the bass and inner parts as separate entities, or are they always a vague background? My experience is that listeners who can mentally separate the various strands of counterpoint in music seldom have much trouble with the other problems of listening. Conversely, those who hear only the top melody clearly usually miss subtle points of form, melodic development, etc. (although they are often strong on colour recognition, and tend to hear all music as a series of dramatic events and climaxes rather than a logical sequence of themes). The ability to hear the lower strands of music is to some extent an inborn gift, though like most gifts it can be enormously increased by the right sort of teaching. I am sure that by far the best way for a person to develop this ability is to learn to sing a lower part in the choir or singing lesson. One thus learns to disregard higher sounds and connect lower sounds up into melody. Also, of course, an appreciation of the power of harmony is born. Indeed, whenever I am asked, as I frequently am, how one can learn to be a better listener, I usually reply in two words, 'Sing alto.' Of course, for 'alto' read 'tenor' or 'bass' if you

are a man. Here's another interesting fact. Among pupils
studying harmony it is usually the boys who do best. The
reason is probably that they can sing bass and can therefore more easily *think bass*. The girls are handicapped by
nature to some extent. (Is this one reason why women
composers are such a small minority?) So valuable training can, and should, be done in the singing lesson. *All
junior schools should attempt two-part singing. All children should
constantly be called on to sing a lower part.* This not only for
many other valuable reasons, but to help train the pupils as
intelligent listeners. Of course, part-playing is the next best
thing. Taking the lower part in recorder playing, or playing
almost any instrument in the orchestra, will help a great deal.

Having made this vital point, let us go on to see what
can be done in the Appreciation lesson to further the pupils'
development as texture listeners. First, make them aware
of the importance of the lower parts. Second, give them
practice in listening to them. Third, show how the knowledge gained can be of use in understanding music.

Here are half a dozen enterprises—I won't call them
courses. Each can occupy anything from one to three
lessons and they can either be taken singly at various
points in the pupils' career, or, with older pupils, strung
together to make one course of about a term's work.

(1) *Types of texture*

Show the pupils (*a*) pure unaccompanied melody, (*b*)
the same melody accompanied by chords. (A good example
of this occurs right at the beginning of Mussorgsky's
Pictures at an Exhibition.) Thus the meaning of *harmony* as a
background is established. The teacher could find one or
two piano pieces with a simple melody and accompaniment, and play the two separately and together. Or he

could find a song which the class have learnt (of the type with a completely independent accompaniment), play the accompaniment only, and ask the class to identify the song. Another point to establish at this stage is the bareness of unaccompanied melody, the way in which it seems to *need* the harmony. Records (or live performances) of folk-songs with guitar will also make this point clearly. So the first type of texture established is *melody and accompaniment*. It may be depicted on the blackboard thus:

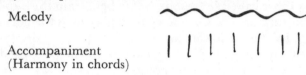

Melody

Accompaniment
(Harmony in chords)

Fig. 1

Next a bass melody can be shown, with chords above it (e.g. parts of Schumann's *Merry Peasant*) and this illustrated as:

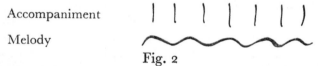

Accompaniment

Melody

Fig. 2

There is a passage in the second movement of Beethoven's Fifth Symphony (bars 98–123) in which we hear the same melody three times: first in the middle register, then on top, finally in the bass. This could be played and the following diagram shown on the board:

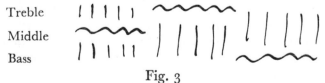

Treble

Middle

Bass

Fig. 3

Now the class should hear the next type of texture—two-part counterpoint. This should be of the pure type—treble and bass only. Bach's Two-part Inventions, Nos. 5, 6, 7, 9, and 11, will serve—or the Gavotte from English Suite No. 3 in G minor. Enough at this stage that the class should be aware that the bass *is a melody*—never mind if they can't follow its exact course. The word 'counterpoint' should be introduced and the following diagram shown:

Treble

Bass

Fig. 4

Next, two-part counterpoint with harmonic accompaniment, e.g. the slow movement of Bach's Concerto for Two Violins.

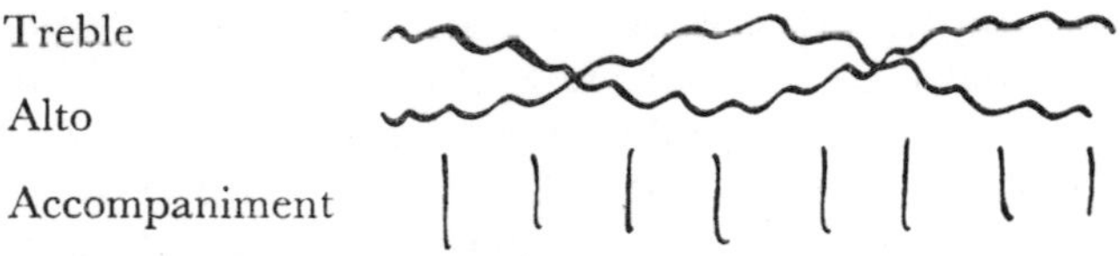

Treble

Alto

Accompaniment

Fig. 5

Or maybe Mozart's 'Bei Männern' (duet from *The Magic Flute*):

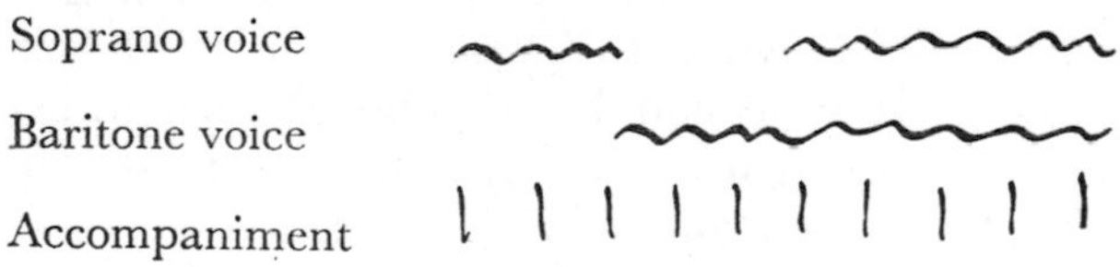

Soprano voice

Baritone voice

Accompaniment

Fig. 6

Lastly, an example of complex counterpoint, e.g. the famous combination of five tunes in the Coda of Mozart's

'Jupiter' Symphony. It will be useless, at this stage, to expect the class to understand or 'follow' this example, and the teacher should attempt no detailed explanation, but so long as the class is aware that all is counterpoint, and no extra harmony is needed, the main point will have been made.

Before going on it may be as well to clear up a doubt which may exist in the reader's mind about harmony and counterpoint. 'Doesn't all harmony produce counterpoint,' he may ask, 'and all counterpoint harmony?' Well, yes, in a way this is true, but it's named according to the emphasis given by the composer and the degree to which it is perceived by the listener. Unless the notes played in the lower parts string themselves together as perceptible and interesting melodies ('horizontal' listening), then we treat them as harmonic accompaniment ('vertical' listening). Only rarely are we in doubt. In many of Bach's chorale harmonisations the lower three parts are of genuine melodic interest (often they are far more interesting than the soprano chorale!), but at the same time the chords produced are so expressive and interesting harmonically that we decide it's a borderline case—'contrapuntal harmony'.

We have made a good start with our basic types, incomplete though they may be, but, of course, there are other, subtler kinds of texture than those mentioned above. They are best dealt with as they occur later on. In fact, this preliminary skirmish could easily be omitted altogether and the types dealt with as they come up. It all depends how much time is available and how thorough you want to be.

(2) *Listening to the bass*

Few activities in music listening are more worth while

than this. The rewards are constant and children can hardly be started on this too early. Let young children be made aware of simple tonic-and-dominant bass parts such as occur in the main part of Verdi's 'La Donna é Mobile' from *Rigoletto*. Let the teacher play the record and double the bass on the piano. The children could join in singing the bass as soon as they learn it (in a higher octave, of course). The same treatment can be given to the middle section of the 'Dance of the Flutes' from Tchaikovsky's *Nutcracker* Suite, where two notes suffice to fit the whole thing. Try juniors with the middle section of the second movement of Tchaikovsky's *Pathetic Symphony*, where the bass is one note, five beats in a bar. Invite them to sing it as soon as they can pick it out. If the previous scheme (types of texture) has not been used, try *The Merry Peasant* or the Beethoven Fifth Symphony examples. It may be also worth while showing the very end of Holst's *Jupiter*, where a fragment of the middle theme occurs momentarily in the bass; particularly if the class have already heard the piece, or learnt the hymn 'I vow to thee, my country'.

Now introduce the pupils to the game of Hidden Tunes invented by Percy Scholes. On the piano, play a tune known to the class with the left hand, and with the right hand play something else. To make it easy for the class, the left hand can be separated from the right by at least an octave, and the right hand will have sustained chords to fit. To make things harder, the right hand plays a counter-melody, or the left hand is brought up closer to the right. I suggest that the teacher should compose his own examples. This way he can be sure that the pupils have a fair chance of success, by picking tunes they have recently learnt. It does not matter if his added counterpoints are badly made. They are not going to be published! So long as the children get their listening practice, this is the main thing. The whole affair should be treated as an enjoyable game; and, say, three such tunes played at each lesson for as many weeks as possible.

When the class is ready for it the next stage is to listen to a Ground Bass or Chaconne. Here a short tune repeats in the bass part while the upper parts keep changing. (Let's clear up some terminology. There is disagreement among authorities, but the following meanings tend to apply: *Ground Bass*: repeating bass theme with a continuous melody, or web of counterpoint, above. The bass theme may appear at different pitches. *Chaconne*: similar to above, but the music is more sectionalised, a new theme or figure being heard above on each repetition of the bass theme. Bass does not normally modulate. *Passacaglia*: same as Chaconne, but bass theme is heard in treble or inner part on some of its appearances, usually later ones.) Attractive Ground Basses are not too easily available, but it would be worth trying Dido's Lament from Purcell's *Dido and Aeneas*, or Pachelbel's *Kanon* (actually a Chaconne), or part of the latter, since it is rather long. Play the bass theme to the class first, and then get them to count the number of bass recurrences. (Be sure to have the correct answer ready!) Another possible Ground Bass is the Crucifixus from Bach's B minor Mass. An elderly gentleman who attended one of my adult classes was quite nonplussed when I pointed out the four-bar chromatic bass theme which is repeated a dozen times in this piece. He literally couldn't hear the theme at all, and went off sadly shaking his head, convinced that I was making it all up. If only he had had the right training in his earlier years!

It is difficult to find much more pure bass listening at

this stage: in most music any theme in the bass is momentary rather than constant; so all we can do now is to pass on, never neglecting to study any bass-theme passages we may come across, and continuing to play Hidden Tunes.

(3) *Listening to inner parts*

This is harder still than listening to the bass, unless the composer has done something special to bring out the tune. Hidden Tunes can again be made, with the theme in the middle of a three-part texture. Play each tune two or three times.

A good exercise in listening to an inner part occurs in Bach's Suite No. 1 for orchestra. Play the last movement, Passepied 1 and 2. The middle section, Passepied 2, has the melody of Passepied 1 now played an octave lower, on violins and violas in unison, while the oboes provide a descant above. The good listener will easily see that the two tunes are identical.

The Passacaglia can be introduced (see above). 'The Death of Falstaff' from Walton's *Henry V* incidental music is a short example. The final variation of Brahms's Variations on the St. Antony Chorale is another, slightly longer. Again the class should be given the theme and invited either to count the total repetitions of it or with older pupils to count the bass appearances separately from those in upper or inner parts. More advanced examples are Bach's Passacaglia in C minor for organ, and the finale of Brahms's Fourth Symphony. The latter is extremely difficult, and should be reserved for advanced pupils, as should the Bach Chaconne in D minor for unaccompanied violin (best heard in Segovia's guitar version). In both these examples the theme is so disguised as to make it useless for normal illustration.

Again, most listening to inner parts will crop up spas-
modically in the normal run of listening. Teachers who
wish to consolidate this and listening to the bass should try
the class with some chamber music. Almost any will do.

(4) *Two-part textures*

When the groundwork of listening to a theme in the bass
or an inner part has been laid, then the pupil should
attempt to hear two tunes at once. This proves a stumbling-
block for many, and lessons involving it should not be
pushed too far if this means that many people will get
discouraged. Nevertheless the capable ones must have their
opportunity.

Bizet's *L'Arlésienne* suites make an attractive start. After
gaining familiarity with the first half of the Prelude from
Suite No. 1, the class should be given the Farandole from
Suite No. 2. Here they will come across the combination
of the two tunes at once. A similar thing happens at the
end of Britten's *The Young Person's Guide to the Orchestra*, and
in Vaughan Williams's Overture to *The Wasps*. In all three
cases two tunes are introduced separately and then combined. Clearer examples of what is meant by *counterpoint*
would be hard to find. The slow movement of Beethoven's
Seventh Symphony could be tried, or at any rate the first
main section. Here there is perhaps the feeling that the
second melody to appear is slightly less important than the
first—a countermelody, in fact. Going back to Passepied 2
from Bach's Suite No. 1, we could listen again, trying to
hear both the oboes and the violins, instead of fiercely
excluding all but the middle voice. (The bass could be
ignored.) Bach, of course, provides almost endless examples
of two-part counterpoint. There are the Two-part Inventions referred to above, or almost any aria with obbligato,

such as No. 3, 'Endlich wird mein Joch', from Cantata
No. 56, *Ich will den Kreuzstab gerne tragen*, a bright piece of
music in which the tones of the bass soloist and the oboe
obbligato are easily distinguished. (It is true that, as in
the Passepied, the continuo bass part actually forms a third
contrapuntal strand, but it is less melodically interesting
than the other two and can be disregarded for our purpose:
in other words we have two-part counterpoint with harmonic accompaniment.) Another delightful Bach piece of
the same type is the Tenor Chorale from Cantata No. 140,
Wachet Auf! (Sleepers Wake). This is best by far in its
original scoring for tenors and strings, although this would
involve buying a record of the entire cantata. It would be
a useful introductory piece, as there are long stretches of
pure melody and the two-part passages are short, so that
the listener's concentration does not have to be sustained
for a long period.

(5) *Canon and imitation*

If the class have learnt any canons in the singing lesson,
they could begin by singing one of them. We must tell them
that it is not (usually) a matter of chance that a tune will
fit in this way—the composer must carefully arrange it so.
If the class divide in two and try to sing 'O God our help'
in canon, this point will soon be made! But of course 'Glory
to thee, my God, this night' will fare better.

Like so many textural devices in music, canon often
occurs without warning in the middle of a piece, and
complete canons suitable for children are hard to find.
The Sarabande from Bach's Suite No. 2 for orchestra has
the bass in canon throughout with the treble, at the inter-
val of the twelfth, but it is a rather difficult example to
follow, especially for beginners. A much clearer example is

the finale of Franck's Violin Sonata. The main theme of
this uses canon at the octave between piano and violin, and
is easily understood. It would be worth hearing the whole
movement, waiting for the canonic theme to reappear.
Another more difficult canon is the opening theme of
Bach's Brandenburg Concerto No. 6. This canon is at the
unison and only a quaver's distance. Examples of short
canonic passages from longer works are Beethoven's Fourth
Symphony, 1st movement, bars 141–57, and Mozart's
Piano Sonata in D, K.576, 1st movement, bars 28–33.

Imitation is short-lived and inexact canon. Madrigals
usually abound with it, and any madrigal recordings that
are to hand will probably furnish several examples. The
Gavotte from Bach's French Suite No. 4 in E♭ is an
excellent example of imitation used in two-part counterpoint. So are Two-part Inventions Nos. 3, 10, 13, and 14.
A study of No. 8 would show one or two pure canonic
passages amidst a welter of imitation. The Scherzo movement of Shostakovich's First Symphony has some passages
of contrapuntal interest. After introducing us to the Trio
theme, the composer shows it in close imitation between
oboes and bassoons. After the recapitulation of the Scherzo
has been made, we hear the Scherzo and Trio themes
simultaneously, and lastly the Trio theme in imitation with
itself against the Scherzo theme.

(6) *Fugue*

In introducing fugue to a class, everything depends on
the age and progress of the pupils. It is fatal to load young
children with too much technical detail. I like to have
several bites at the apple, introducing fugue early on in
very simple terms, and returning to it at various times
later, adding more information each time. In a first lesson

the class can be told that the voices or instruments come in one after the other with the same tune, and when they're all in, they take further turns at the tune for the rest of the composition. This is, after all, all that really matters about a fugue at this stage and for a long time to come. Pupils should from now on hear fugues as often as possible, without the need for the teacher to feel that he must explain everything that is going on. The second stage of explanation concerns itself with the contrapuntal nature of the whole thing—the fact that we never get chordal accompaniment, but there is always melody in all the voices. At a third stage maybe episodes and stretti are pointed out, and later still, if the pupils are interested, the tonic and dominant entries at the beginning, and such things as augmentation, inversion and pedal.

Bach again is the chief source of material. If the teacher can play one of the '48' at the piano and analyse it with comments, this will be of immense value. No. 2 in C minor from Book 1 makes a very suitable start. The well-known organ Toccata and Fugue in D minor does not actually provide a very typical fugue and is best avoided for teaching purposes. Lively fugues are found in the overtures to Bach's four orchestral suites. Other useful examples are Vivaldi's Concerto in D minor, Op. 3, No. 11 (*L'Estro Armonico*), 3rd movement; Handel's Oboe Concerto No. 2 in B♭, 2nd movement; his Concerto Grosso No. 5 in D, 2nd movement, and 'And with his stripes' from *Messiah*; the final variation of Dohnanyi's *Variations on a Nursery Song*, and the fugue from Britten's *Young Person's Guide*. Really advanced pupils should try the first movements of Beethoven's String Quartet in C sharp minor, Op. 131, and of Bartók's Music for Strings, Percussion, and Celesta.

Having surveyed several important facets of textural listening, let me emphasise that the good teacher does not stop there. He keeps the attention of his pupils constantly on listening to lower parts whenever there is something to be gained by doing so, in whatever piece is being studied—and this goes for the singing lesson as well as the listening lesson. It is indeed obvious enough to most teachers that children's attention should be drawn to the 'leaping fish' figure in the accompaniment to Schubert's 'The Trout', but how many have bothered with the bass part of Purcell's 'Nymphs and Shepherds'? (This bass line was, of course, the only accompaniment provided by the composer; the other notes given are an editorial continuo realisation.) In the second half of this song we have a beautiful example of free imitation: the voice part and the bass make a splendid contrapuntal pair. Study the piece and see.

Another obvious link-up is the Aural Training lesson. The use of two-part dictation or the writing down of simple chords is enormously helpful in training the kind of listening we want. One point occurs to me here: why do we always play melodies for dictation in soprano range? Why not two octaves lower sometimes, particularly to get girls to listen to low sounds? And for that matter we should play tests in all sorts of registers from very low to very high.

Score reading was mentioned in the last chapter. Provided that the pupils have had some practice in it, it can be extremely useful as a help in any of the activities mentioned above. But it is most important that the class should be fluent enough at reading not to flounder. We want their attention on contrapuntal listening, remember; not on a frantic searching for the place.

Before ending this chapter I must point out the enormous usefulness of the piano in teaching how to listen to texture. Not only in the game of Hidden Tunes, but to illustrate every point that we have come across, the teacher's personal touch at the piano is invaluable. One device I often use is to bring out an inner or bass part of a piece by doubling it on the piano while a record is playing. Needless to say, I make sure first that the gramophone and piano are in tune with one another (also that I know exactly what to play!). This device should not be overdone, though. Having made my point, I quickly withdraw and hope that the class will be able to follow the thread I have drawn attention to.

4. Teaching Form

If ability to hear tunes in lower voices is the test of the good listener, then musical form is an aspect of listening which can be understood by all except the tone-deaf. If I had to confine myself to one approach only, I would teach form as combining importance with comprehensibility, and it is surely the approach which the listener most *needs to be taught*—he is unlikely to discover much about form if left to his own devices. However, it is not all easy and plain sailing for the student. His most important faculty is memory, without which he'll never make much sense of musical form. The ability to recognise a theme when it recurs after the lapse of some time is a fundamental necessity for the listener. Fortunately few people have any trouble here. It is the next step which may undo us: Can we recognise a theme in disguise? And let's put the matter a little differently: do we take *pleasure* in hearing themes come round again (in exactly the same form)? And do we *enjoy* hearing them in a modified form, or does this confuse or irritate us? We must realise that the ability to enjoy simple repetition is basic to a love of music, and that enjoyment of disguised repetition is a more sophisticated attitude. Let us have patience with those who cannot easily make the step from one to the other. Once a theme can be recognised on all its later appearances, the principles of design can be grasped. *And it is more important for the listener to grasp the principles than to learn technical names without real understanding.* The main principle of form has been stated often enough: it is Variety within Unity. Variety and Unity are opposites, of course, and composers have to avoid the two extremes of constant and exact repetition on the one hand and constant meandering on the other. Provided they can strike a reasonable balance between the two, the problem of form may well be solved. I say 'may well be' because there is no ready-made formula for success. Music is like a living thing during composition and finds its own best form. The teacher must beware of thinking that there is some magic virtue in the form itself which ensures quality. When a piece appears to defy the 'laws' of form, remember that the great composers came first and the textbooks after; our job is to describe what exists, not to say what ought to exist. I make no apology for labouring this oft-made point: it cannot be made too often. A music teacher shocked me badly once by grumbling that a G.C.E. examining board had set for study Mozart's Piano Sonata in D, K. 311, in the first movement of which the second subject is recapitulated before the first subject. 'What is the use,' he moaned, 'of teaching kids all about Sonata form if the examiners are going to do things like this? Now I've got to upset all their ideas.' At my suggestion that his teaching hadn't yet gone far enough, and that he ought to be grateful to the examiners for the opportunity thus given, he was simply incredulous. And this was a Bachelor of Music! But it was in his younger days, and I like to hope he's learned better since.

Our aim in teaching the various forms, Binary, Ternary, and so on, is not so that the pupil can take each piece he hears and put it in the right pigeon-hole like a postal sorter; but so that he can grasp principles from them, and if he sees the principles differently applied, understand the way this is done.

Returning once more to the twin pillars of Variety and Unity, let me point out that there are only two ways they can be used in a piece, plus a third way of combining the methods:

(1) State a theme, digress, and return to it.
(2) State a theme and restate it in a different form.
(3) State a theme, digress, and return to it in a different form.

(Also, for 'in a different form' we might read 'in a different context'.)

Reduced to the letters beloved of analysts (I love them, too, actually) we get:

(1) A B A
(2) A A^1
(3) A B A^1

Out of these three ways and their logical extensions we get all other forms. (I leave it to the reader to work out why and how.) It is because of this last fact that I prefer to begin a study of musical form with an exploration of the principles behind it, maybe spreading over weeks of study. Quite young children will enjoy counting recurrences of themes, or putting up their hands when the main theme returns. Other ideas are (1) putting up right hand when theme is unchanged, and left hand when it is disguised; (2) dividing the class according to the number of important themes. Each section puts up hands when its theme appears. Folk-songs and other simple tunes known to the children make a good starting-point. The teacher had perhaps better avoid the use of the words Binary,

Ternary, etc., in connexion with these tunes. Rondos, Minuets, and Trios and pieces in Sonata form lend themselves to this game. Variations can be shown, and although the class cannot participate in quite the same way, they should enjoy listening to simple examples, especially if the teacher knows enough composition to knock up a set of variations on one of their favourite songs, as a starting-point. Juniors are quite able to learn Simple Rondo, Variations, and Ternary form (but the latter only in its larger manifestations, see (3) and (5) below; not the Simple Ternary with repeats. At this stage call them all Ternary.) These forms will need revising at senior level, but no matter.

A senior course might run:

(1) Basic principles of form
(2) Simple Ternary form
(3) Da Capo form and Episodical form
(4) Simple Rondo
(5) Minuet and Trio, Scherzo and Trio
(6) Binary form
(7) Variations
(8) Introductions and Codas: Revision
(9) Sonata form
(10) Deviations from Sonata form
(11) Sonata-Rondo form

To the above could be added a supplementary course, if there is time:

(12) General plan of Sonata, Symphony, etc., giving accurate definitions of these and other words such as quartet, concerto, etc.
(13) Examination of Concerto form at various periods.

(14) The eighteenth-century suite and the different dance forms comprising it.

Fiske's *Score-reading, Book 2, Musical Form* will be useful, but does not cover all the forms mentioned. *Book 3, Concertos* covers (13) above very well.

(Before going any further I must mention the question of key in music: or more specifically, the recognition of keys and key changes by the listener. How important is this? Well, frankly, I don't think it is absolutely vital to an understanding of musical form. It is perfectly possible for a child to understand forms from the point of view of thematic planning without an understanding of key. How many professional musicians and teachers can follow the key changes in what they hear, without seeing the score? I hasten to add that I do not consider training in key recognition undesirable—far from it—but it is best dealt with in the Aural Training lesson: where it crops up in the Appreciation lesson it can be *referred to* and a certain amount of incidental training attempted (with pupils aged, say, 14 and over), but the matter should not be allowed to hold up the main teaching programme.)

There follow my suggestions for records and piano pieces, together with a good many warnings which experience has proved necessary. I will deal only with the first eleven suggestions on the above list.

(1) *Basic principles of form*

For theme counting:

 Haydn: Trumpet Concerto, finale
 Mozart: Horn Concerto No. 4, finale
 Mozart: Viennese Sonatina No. 1, 4th movement
 Beethoven: *Sonata Pathétique*, 2nd movement
 Poulenc: *Mouvements Perpétuels*, No. 1

For theme counting with disguised theme:

> Beethoven: Symphony No. 5, 2nd movement
> Tchaikovsky: *Nutcracker* ('Sugar Plum Fairy' and 'Arabian Dance')
> Prokofiev: *Peter and the Wolf* (extracts)

For simple variations:

> Handel: 'The Harmonious Blacksmith'
> Haydn: 'Emperor' String Quartet, 2nd movement
> Haydn: 'Surprise' Symphony, 2nd movement

(2) *Simple Ternary form*

Although A B A without repeats is possible (e.g. 'Dance of the Sugar Plum Fairy') it is far less common than the normal A :‖: BA :‖ so much used by the classical composers. A may or may not modulate to the dominant key. B may be new or may be derived from A, but in any case does not normally offer a *sharp* contrast to A—it goes on more or less in the same style. The last A is seldom exactly the same as the first: the main thing is that it should make us feel we have returned to the first idea in the tonic key. The listener's problem is that he hears A A B A B A and *must learn to disregard repeats*, thus finding three sections and giving the word 'ternary' its justification.

> Mozart: 'Haffner' Symphony, Minuet without Trio
> Beethoven: Sonata in A, Op. 2, No. 2, Scherzo without Trio
> Beethoven: Sonata in A♭, Op. 26, 1st movement (theme only)
> Schumann: 'Cradle Song', 'Soldier's March', and 'Merry Peasant'
> Chopin: Mazurka in A minor, Op. 7, No. 2 (first part in A minor only)

(3) *Da Capo and Episodical forms*

Here we have pieces which, although clearly of the Ternary family, have A or B sections which are on the one hand too long and involved to come under the category of simple Ternary, and on the other hand are not organised enough to merit the title of Minuet and Trio form. Repeats, an almost invariable feature of simple Ternary form, will generally be missing.

Da Capo:

> Handel: 'Where'er you walk', from *Semele*
>   'Art thou troubled', from *Rodelinda*
>   'He was despised', from *Messiah*

Episodical:

> Mozart: Clarinet Quintet, slow movement
> Chopin: Prelude No. 15 in Db
> Grieg: Piano Concerto, slow movement
> Tchaikovsky: *Nutcracker* ('March' and 'Dance of the Flutes')

(4) *Simple Rondo*

Sometimes called Old Rondo, this should be one of the easiest forms to understand, but only if the examples are carefully chosen. It is worth noting that often the main theme and the episodes are each in Binary or Ternary form, so that the whole effect could be regarded as an extension of the Minuet and Trio idea. An example of this is the finale to Haydn's Sonata in D for Pianoforte, where the plan is:

> A :‖: BA :‖: C :‖: DC :‖: A :‖: BA :‖: E :‖: FE :‖ Link ‖: A :‖: BA :‖

It is perhaps best to avoid these at first or confusion might result if pupils are looking only for repetitions of A and the teacher is looking for repetitions of A :||: BA :||. Indeed confusion in teaching form often arises because it is not easy to lay down what is the length of the 'section' under consideration. Imagine you are a pupil and the teacher asks you to find how many sections there are in a given piece. You might find twenty-four where he finds three. Or you might still be in section 1 when the piece ends. So with Rondos it's best to demonstrate first what is meant by the main theme before asking for later recognition of it. A typical case of this confusion might arise from Beethoven's *Für Elise*. The main theme is ternary (with repeats the first time), but the episodes are not (A :||: BA :|| C | ABA | D | ABA). Now, you and I are perfectly capable of reducing this to A | B | A | C | A, since we take the main theme to be one unit, but we must also be capable of understanding the pupil who thinks he hears the main theme eight times, or even six, since immediate repeats should be disregarded. Work it out! On the other hand, the trouble may never arise. There is a strong feeling of unity between the A and B of the main theme which help to make them digestible in one mouthful, as it were, and the class may see it easily. But perhaps it's better not to risk it, especially when introducing the subject. Clarke's Trumpet Voluntary is a bit more foolproof as a starting-point, although even this has a concealed danger of the opposite nature. The B section is so much in the style of A that we might perform the following mental mathematics:

$$We\ hear\ A\ B\ A\ C\ A$$
$$but\ A\ B\ A = A$$
$$\therefore\ A\ B\ A\ C\ A = A\ C\ A\ [i.e.\ A\ B\ A]$$
$$= Ternary$$
$$Q.N.E.D.$$

To avoid this danger the teacher should first play the main theme before giving the whole piece. Alternatively he can give the analysis verbally whilst the piece is in progress.

Reasonably safe Rondos:

Bach: Gavotte from Suite in E for unaccompanied violin (or in guitar version)
Finale of Violin Concerto in E
Ravel: *Pavane pour une Infante Défunte*

Slightly risky Rondos:

Clarke: Trumpet Voluntary
Bach: Rondeau from Suite No. 2 for orchestra
Mozart: Viennese Sonatina No. 1, finale
Beethoven: *Für Elise*

A more difficult Rondo:

Mozart: Rondo in A minor, for pianoforte

So-called 'rondos' which do *not* exemplify the form:

Haydn: Trumpet Concerto, finale
Mozart: Rondo in D for piano; Rondo alla Turca from Sonata in A; Horn Concerti, finales
(and probably every Mozart and Beethoven finale headed 'Rondo'. They are usually in Sonata-Rondo form.)
Strauss: *Till Eulenspiegel* (subtitled 'in rondo form')

(5) *Minuet and Trio*

Of course, the origin of this form lies in the desire to create a longer piece from existing music, by putting two pieces together. Since both pieces are probably Ternary in themselves the net result:

A	B	A
Minuet	Trio	Minuet
a :‖: b a :‖	c :‖: d c :‖	a ‖ b a

is seen to be ternary within ternary, or 'ternary squared' as I like to put it to older pupils. (Of course, either minuet or trio could be binary.) With younger pupils I pretend that the dancers used to complain to the band that one, or even two, dances were not long enough to make it worth while going on to the dance floor. Three dances were too long and tiring, so the third dance had its repeats omitted. It was the lazy musicians' idea to play the first minuet again instead of a third one, to save finding another piece! (And, of course, because the resulting form is better.) Outrageous fiction like this does not worry my conscience a great deal. Anyway, can anyone prove it untrue? The main thing is that we are seeking reasons and principles and helping to make matters more memorable to the pupils. Both younger and older children can, of course, be told that the word 'trio' originated from the three instruments originally used to give the ear a relief in the middle. In any case the Trio usually offers a contrast of style and key, and this should be pointed out.

Examples abound in classical music. The following have been found to have strong appeal:

Haydn: 'Clock' Symphony, No. 101 in D, 3rd movement
Mozart: *Eine Kleine Nachtmusik*, 3rd movement
    Symphony No. 39 in E♭, 3rd movement
Beethoven: Minuet in G

Note that many other pieces besides minuets use the same form. When this occurs we apply the term Minuet and Trio form, whatever the style of music involved. The exception, for some reason, is the Scherzo and Trio, although there is no difference in the basic layout.

Scherzos:

Beethoven: Symphonies Nos. 1 and 3, 3rd movements

Piano Sonatas Op. 2, Nos. 2 and 3, 3rd movements
Schubert: Scherzo in B♭ for piano
Dvořák: 'New World' Symphony, 3rd movement

Other pieces:

Bach: Gavotte and Musette from English Suite No. 3 in
    G minor (the Gavotte is binary)
Chopin: Waltz in D♭
    Polonaise in A
Grieg: Four Norwegian Dances
Kodály: Intermezzo from *Háry János* (both sections are
    binary)

(6) *Binary form*

One of the biggest mistakes a teacher can make is to
imagine that because a binary piece can be put down on
paper as A B it is the easiest form to recognise by ear.
Nothing could be farther from the truth. It is one of the
hardest, for various reasons: (*a*) Its length can vary
enormously. Compare Purcell's well-known little Air in D
minor (16 bars not counting repeats) with the last movement of Bach's Brandenburg Concerto No. 3 (48 bars of
$\frac{12}{8}$, really equivalent to 96 bars of $\frac{6}{8}$, nearly all of which
have 12 fast-moving notes to the bar). (*b*) Since the title
'binary' means divided into two parts, everything depends
on the effect of the cadence at the double bar. Can this be
heard? The matter is full of pitfalls. In attempting to
demonstrate this twofold division I once, as a young
teacher, unwisely chose Handel's Minuet 1 in F (from
Seven Pieces) and asked the class to put up their hands
when they felt a strong cadence. All went well at the
double bar, but I was crestfallen when hands went up

half-way through the second section. The boys were right
—there is a strong cadence there, in the relative minor.
So now the piece was in three sections, but not ternary,
for it was A B C! Bang went my lesson on Binary form,
but at least I had learned the importance of looking more
carefully at my examples before using them as demonstra-
tions. Are we then to rely on repeats to identify Binary
form? If so, we must be careful not to confuse it with
Ternary form. And does a binary minuet become 'unitary'
when recapitulated without repeats? (c) The second
section of a binary piece often begins by using the opening
figure in the dominant key. Surely a pupil can be forgiven
for reasoning that he has heard A (the opening theme),
B (the rest of first section), A (beginning of second section),
C (rest of second section) = Ternary with Coda?

Of course, the answers to all these problems lie in the
matter of key. But please never forget that whilst the
teacher (perhaps with a copy before him) may know what
key the music is at a given moment, it requires a strongly
developed sense of tonality in the listener to make much
of key-relationships, however clear the composer has tried
to be. This appreciation of key comes only after much
practice; and good teaching is needed, both in and out of
the Appreciation class, to make the pupil aware of its
reality and importance. Therefore I regard a thorough
understanding of Binary form as a matter for the advanced
student. The younger pupil should know of its existence,
but simple examples, carefully chosen, will suffice. Better
to avoid the problems created by the internal organisation
of Binary form until a later stage. (But they will have to be
faced as soon as it occurs to an intelligent pupil to ask
where is the unity in a binary piece—so have your answer
ready!)

Simple examples:

Byrd: Pavane and Galliard, *The Earl of Salisbury*
Bach: Gavotte from French Suite No. 5
    Bourrée No. 2 from English Suite No. 2 (also as recorded
        by Swingle Singers)
Mozart: Minuet from *Don Giovanni* (if it can be found in a
    piano arrangement)

More difficult:

Bach: French Suite No. 5 (remaining pieces)
Handel: Prelude in G (from Seven Pieces)
Scarlatti: Tempo di ballo (Sonata in D)

(7) *Variations*

Some suggestions suitable for young children have been
made above, under paragraph (1). With older pupils, the
teacher must make up his mind whether he is going to be
content merely to point out the existence of the form and
play some examples, or whether he is going to explain the
various ways in which variations are carried out. This is
well worth while if there is time, as there are only four
basic methods, and the first two at least are reasonably
easy to understand. The methods are:

(1) Decoration of the melody. Its features are altered,
usually by adding extra notes, but the skeleton melody can
always be seen (and heard) underneath.

(2) Keeping the melody intact, but changing the
accompaniment so that it offers new harmonic or contrapuntal interest. This process may involve putting the
melody into a lower part.

(3) Keeping the harmony (more or less) intact, but
creating a new melody. The phrasing and form of the
original will be preserved.

(4) Free treatment, losing the exact proportions of the original. This is closely akin to *development*, but as it often occurs in sets of variations, it must be included here.

Note carefully that, while changes in time, tempo, mode, dynamics, register, key, or instrumentation may also be made, these are not true variation methods in themselves, but will accompany one of the above and be subsidiary to it.

Method No. (3) can be somewhat baffling in practice, and if the question 'Where is the tune?' cannot be answered, then usually the harmony is the same. A good test is to play or sing the original melody over the variation. It should fit (at any rate most of the time), and if it doesn't, then the answer is—it isn't a variation at all! It does sometimes happen that a composer slips into a set of variations what is actually an episode. There are two such episodes in the variation-finale of Mozart's Piano Concerto in C minor, K.491, for example; and 'Dorabella' in the 'Enigma' Variations is not a variation, although headed 'X' in the score (tenth variation). One final point worth noting is that in most cases the theme taken for variations (at any rate in classical music) will be in Binary or Ternary form; and so, therefore, will all the variations.

Example of Method (1):

Mozart: Piano Sonata in A, K. 331, 1st movement (omit Variation 3)

Examples of Method (2):

Haydn: 'Emperor' String Quartet, slow movement
Bizet: *L'Arlésienne* Suite No. 1, Prelude (first half)

Example of Method (3):

Brahms: St. Antony Variations (all but last variation)

Examples of Method (4):

Elgar: 'Enigma' Variations
Britten: *Young Person's Guide to the Orchestra* (very free)

Example showing all the methods:

Arensky: Variations on a theme of Tchaikovsky

Other useful sets, some of an extended and free nature:

Schubert: 'Trout' Quintet, 4th movement
Beethoven: 'Eroica' Symphony, finale
Tchaikovsky: Theme and Variations from Suite in G
Dohnanyi: Variations on a Nursery Theme (this may be
    on a nursery theme, but the variations are very sophisti-
    cated and mostly unsuitable for young children)
Rachmaninov: Rhapsody on a theme of Paganini

(8) *Introductions and Codas*

Pupils will readily understand that a 'lead-in' or
'rounding-off' section makes no difference to the basic
form of a piece. In introducing this point I like to spend
most of the lesson on a revision test, involving aural recognition of the forms already known. Half a dozen short
pieces are played and the class must write down the form
of each, stating whether there is an introduction or a coda.
(We do not count a few bars 'vamp till ready' as an introduction.)

A few examples of short pieces with Introductions and
Codas are given here. For pieces without them, refer to
earlier lists.

Episodical:

Mozart: Larghetto from Clarinet Quintet (Coda)
Vaughan Williams: *Fantasia on Greensleeves* (Introduction)

Rondo:

> Haydn: *Gipsy Rondo* (Coda)
> Beethoven: *Sonata Pathétique*, slow movement (Coda)

Minuet and Trio:

> Chopin: Waltz in E minor (both)
> Tchaikovsky: 'Flower Waltz' from *Nutcracker* (both)

Variations:

> Beethoven: Andante from Sonata in G, Op. 14, No. 2
> (short Coda)

(9) *Sonata form*

This vital key to the understanding of so many hundreds of pieces should be taken seriously and taught carefully. It is best approached as an expansion of Ternary form (which it is, historically) and the subdivisions of the outer sections explained. Now some warnings: (*a*) Remember that a piece in textbook Sonata form, like the average man, is difficult to find. Emphasise, right from the start, that the plan being shown is one that pieces *tend* to stick to, but that each will probably have individual features. Mozart is one of the most dangerous composers to use as an illustration: contrary to the opinion of many, he is *not* the archetype of the formal and symmetrical composer. Beethoven comes nearer to being that! However, there is one, and only one, well-known Mozart piece which it is safe to use as a textbook example of Sonata form: the first movement of *Eine Kleine Nachtmusik*. Even here the Development is very rudimentary, but that is all to the good for our purpose. I invariably use this piece as an introduction to Sonata form, and can think of none better, provided we immediately follow it by other pieces in more elastic versions of the form, so that the pupil understands the freedom open to the composer. (*b*) Be sure about Bridge Passages (Transitions). Remember they start in the tonic key, and often use the first subject to begin with. What we think to be a repeat of the first subject will nearly always turn out to be the Bridge. (See the *Egmont* Overture, for instance.) (*c*) Don't make a fuss about the so-called Codetta or Closing Section. After all, it is only the final theme of the Second Subject. Why single it out, unless it clearly has an air of rounding-off? In most cases it is better to forget it, or rather to treat it as another theme in the Second Subject group. It is certainly untrue to say that an Exposition consists of four sections: First Subject, Bridge, Second Subject, and Closing Section. I repeat, the Closing Section is part of the Second Subject. (*d*) The Coda, of course, is an optional extra, not an integral part of the form. When present it should be regarded as a separate, fourth main section, not as an extension to the Recapitulation.

Examples of Sonata form are so numerous that the choice is bewildering. Here are a few of the more straightforward. It is wise to present at least three of these before leaving the topic.

Mozart: *Eine Kleine Nachtmusik*, 1st movement
    Symphony No. 40 in G minor, 1st and last movements
Beethoven: Symphonies Nos. 1 and 2, 1st and last movements
    Sonata Op. 2, No. 1, 1st movement
Mendelssohn: *Hebrides* Overture
Grieg: Piano Concerto, 1st movement

(10) *Deviations from Sonata form*

A lesson devoted to these will serve to underline the freedom of the composer referred to in the previous section.

The teacher will use as many of these as he thinks expedient. Perhaps only the first is important.

(a) Abridged Sonata form (Development omitted):

Mozart: *Marriage of Figaro* Overture
Beethoven: Sonata Op. 2, No. 1, 2nd movement
Rossini: *Barber of Seville* Overture
  Thieving Magpie Overture
Tchaikovsky: Miniature Overture, *Nutcracker* Suite

(b) Development containing an Episode:

Beethoven: 'Eroica' Symphony, 1st movement

(c) Episode instead of Development:

Mozart: Symphony No. 29 in A, 1st movement
Grieg: Piano Concerto, finale

(d) Themes omitted from Recapitulation
(e) Second Subject using theme of First Subject:

Mozart: Oboe Quartet, 1st movement, provides an example of each of the three foregoing points.

(f) Exposition contains some Development:

Beethoven: Symphony No. 5, 1st movement
Schubert: Unfinished Symphony, 1st movement

(11) *Sonata-Rondo form*

A warning has already been given that Mozart and Beethoven nearly always head their finale movements with the one word 'Rondo' when using this form.

Useful examples:

Mozart: Horn Concerto No. 4, finale (although the Second Subject is varied in the Recapitulation)
Beethoven: *Sonata Pathétique*, finale

I began this chapter by emphasising the importance of the subject of musical form. I must end, however, with another warning, especially if the teacher is particularly fascinated by the subject. Formal analysis of music must never become, or seem to the pupil to become, an end in itself. It is only a way to a better understanding of music. In the last resort an encyclopedic knowledge of form in all its aspects is useless in making anyone love music. Only, then, in so far as it may help to create a love or understanding of music should it be taught at all.

5. Teaching History

This subject is fraught with dangers. Scylla and Charybdis await us: on the one hand in being informative we may bore; on the other hand in being interesting we may tell nothing worth knowing. Yet again there is no guarantee that steering a middle course will get us out of troubled waters. The two main possible approaches to the teaching of music history are (1) teaching about composers, the facts of their lives, and so on; (2) teaching about music, the different forms it has taken according to social conditions, etc. Now, it seems to me that the second of these is the only one that really matters, since we are trying to teach understanding of *music*, first and foremost. On the other hand, it tends to interest only the more advanced, and perhaps the more intellectually minded, of our pupils. The first method usually throws little direct light on music, but it tends to be more interesting, especially to younger children, or even to adults not well gifted in purely musical perception. In the strict sense, facts about composers such as whether they married, how old they were when they went to music college, or even what instrument they played, are useless in helping us to understand and appreciate their music. Much more to the point is to learn what were the musical practices of the day, what aspects of music were considered important, what new contributions each composer made to the evolution of music. Perhaps, to be perfectly strict, even these facts don't really help either. Ultimately the music itself must be studied in its own terms, but the latter approach surely comes nearer to this. Let the reader judge which of these facts throws most light on Bach's music:

(1) When young he copied his brother's manuscript by moonlight.
(2) He used to quarrel with the Leipzig authorities.
(3) His concerted music needs a continuo instrument, such as the organ, to fill out the harmony and hold the music together.
(4) His music is dominated by a contrapuntal habit of thought.

Surely these facts are given in order of growing importance?

However, it would be extremely foolish to overlook the matter of *human interest*. Considered from a child's point of view, the above facts are just as surely in order of decreasing interest. One fact about teaching Musical Appreciation must never be lost sight of: *interest must first be aroused before teaching can follow*. So the technique of teaching the History of Music lies in being (1) as usefully informative as possible, (2) as humanly interesting as necessary. The age and progress of the pupils decides the blend of the two. So, for example, of the above facts about Bach, I would teach (1) to children aged 8–12, (2) to children aged 12–14, (3) to children aged 14–16, and (4) to children aged 16 and over. But I might well start at (2) or even (1) with inexperienced adults of any age!

Now, how do we work out a scheme of teaching History of Music? Well, it will be clear from the above that young children need anecdotes, of almost any kind, to help identify composers as human beings and not just as names on a piece of music. For example, young Bach tramping miles and finding the fish-heads, Handel practising in the attic, Haydn cutting off his brother's pigtail, Mozart writing Allegri's *Miserere* from memory, Beethoven being arrested as a tramp, Mendelssohn visiting Fingal's Cave, Brahms playing with children, etc. But let's face it: unless you're better stocked up with such stories than I am, it won't be long before you run out. Such things only prick the surface of the subject, and are only of use for dropping in along with the presentation of some record or piano piece. One can't, and shouldn't, make a whole lesson out of them. The most important thing of all is for the child to acquire, bit by bit, a knowledge of actual music. Never forget that music is the beginning and end of our study, and music means *sound*. All else is subsidiary to this. The best foundation for a History of Music, as with any other approach to Musical Appreciation, is to build up a 'listener's repertoire' of suitable pieces. The fact is that one is more likely to become interested in a composer *after* one has found pleasure in his music. Surely few people, if any, become interested first in composers, then in their music?

For pupils who are ready for it, say aged 9–14 depending on intelligence and interest, a course can be worked out in which composers are presented one at a time, with examples of their music. Such basic facts as are important should be given, but the fewer the better. Dates of birth and death are inevitable, I suppose, but it is doubtful whether children should be expected to learn them by heart. How each composer made his living can be mentioned, and his chief types of composition; e.g. Haydn was employed by a prince to provide him with orchestral music, and thus we have his symphonies. A number of lessons such as this will build up in the pupil's mind an aggregate of knowledge about important composers. This will not amount to a 'History of Music', but it will prove to be the next important step after the establishing of the foundational repertoire.

A course for 14–16-year-olds would have a short list of really important works by each composer. These should be memorised as far as possible. Needless to say the teacher chooses his illustrations from the list. For example, in a lesson on Brahms we could give the following:

4 symphonies
Concertos (2 for piano, 1 for violin, 1 for violin and cello)
Academic Festival Overture
Tragic Overture
German Requiem
Variations on the St. Antony Chorale

What records are played depends on the teacher's taste. There would, perhaps, be time for, say, the St. Antony Variations and the finale of the Violin Concerto.

In teaching pupils aged 16 or over, we would probably be dealing only with G.C.E. A level candidates. Here a much more thorough grounding is necessary, the exact terms of which may be dictated by examination requirements. But assuming no particular shackles, and also assuming an existing skeleton knowledge of composers and some of their works, the emphasis would now be much more on the exact nature of the contribution of each composer to music—his individual style, his innovations, his particular gifts. 'Schools' of composition would be mentioned, and the influence of one composer on another. Pupils would learn at what stages in history counterpoint and harmony began, when and why opera was invented, how Sonata form came into being, the different methods of performance and the different instruments which have been used, how chamber music developed, and so on. There is literally no end to the fascinating byways that can be explored by anyone who is really interested in musical history: of course, a study of them can extend into adult life, *indeed should extend into the teacher's own life*. How far do we take the pupil? This question is a difficult one to answer. Again I must warn about Scylla and Charybdis, and again I must urge the teacher to take both his own and his pupils' progress and interest into consideration.

Another matter which must be mentioned is applicable, to a greater or less extent, at all stages. The History of Music should be related to other history. It is insufficient to show what is going on in music alone—what about the social conditions of the time, and what about the history of the other arts of painting, architecture, literature, and drama? A music teacher who taught about early opera purely from a musical point of view would be throwing away a first-class opportunity to talk about all of these other things. So the customary wall chart of strips showing composers' lives should as far as possible include, perhaps underneath, strips for great artists and writers, besides showing the reigning English monarch. With young pupils such anecdotes as Handel quarrelling with King George, or Mozart promising to marry Marie Antoinette, will provide helpful links.

Let me now enumerate some possible reasons which may be given for teaching the History of Music:

(1) To show how music evolved through its various stages.
(2) To show the relation between music and society at different times.

(3) To show who were the most important creators of music, i.e. the great composers and performers.

(4) To establish links between composers and their works, i.e. to show who wrote what.

(5) To teach facts about composers, or their music, which may be important, or interesting, or both.

(6) To familiarise pupils with various musical styles, so as to lay the foundation for a catholic taste.

(7) To explain whatever may be necessary to facilitate understanding of styles and aims which may differ from period to period.

(8) As an excuse for letting pupils hear music, in the hope that they may come to love it.

I believe all of the above to be good and proper reasons. Which is the most important I would not care to say. The reader may choose his own—in fact, the reader *should* choose his own. One must teach what one believes in. It does not matter that a certain bias will thus be given to the teaching: it will, at any rate, probably be done well, and certainly with conviction. Read on now—pick about among the following oddments, remnants, and genuine bargains. Somewhere there may be one which appeals to you—an approach you think you could put over. These, then, are some possible branches of history teaching:

(1) Keyboard music from the sixteenth to the twentieth centuries.

(2) The history of violin music.

(3) Great piano composers.

(4) How the orchestra grew.

(5) The history of chamber music.

(6) Vocal music through the ages.

(7) Church music.

(8) Opera.

(9) Story music from different centuries.

(10) Ballet music of all times.

(11) The symphony.

(12) The concerto.

(13) The overture.

(14) Stories of young composers.

(15) Some famous composer-performers.

(16) A history of musical form.

(17) Musical patrons throughout the ages.

(18) Theatre, film, and television music.

(19) Twenty masterpieces from Purcell to Britten.

(20) The development of harmony.

This, of course, is not an exhaustive list. But how many of us even have time to teach all of the above? Normally we have to choose as many as we feel we can cope with. They will not necessarily be taught separately. A complete History of Music would include all these, and others, running parallel: we may naturally be unable to be as complete as this, but could easily run several topics alongside each other.

I cannot end this chapter without raising a most important matter. Modern music should be included in every scheme. It is a poor sort of 'history' which does not come up to the present day and show the student living history. Indeed, it has often been pointed out that one of the peculiarities of our age is that we listen mainly to music of the past, whereas our forefathers always listened to modern music, i.e. the music of their own day. This is not to say that we should avoid listening to classical music, but to urge that tastes should be catholic. What if the teacher's taste is not catholic? I have stressed above that the teacher should teach what he believes in. What if he genuinely cannot like or understand modern music? Had he better not avoid it? No—this is one case where the teacher really must make the effort to give his pupils what he lacks himself. Young people are not born with any particular musical taste. Their tastes will be formed by whatever they come into contact with. Now is the time to form them: later they will be like you and every other adult—they will find it difficult or impossible to change the taste formed in youth. We owe it to our pupils, then, to let them hear *every* kind of good music. All right, you say, we'll have *Firebird* or *Rite of Spring*, or even Schönberg's *Five Orchestral Pieces* for older pupils. Fine! Congratulations, so you should. *Now you're only half a century behind the times.* And please don't imagine that playing *Peter and the Wolf* or *Young Person's Guide* will bring you more up to date. In style they are earlier than the first examples. What, then, do I want? Well, naming actual examples of bang-up-to-date music would defeat its own purpose: by the time this book has been in print a year or two, they won't *be* up to date. Let the teacher find out new trends and keep up with them himself. It doesn't follow, of course, that everything will be religiously passed on to the pupils. In any case they need only a reasonably small ration of modern music; and one is at the mercy of the recording companies to a large extent. But let us not forget, or let our pupils forget, that music is a living and growing art, not a series of museum exhibits.

6. Planning the Work

In previous chapters I have outlined the four main approaches in teaching Musical Appreciation—Colour, Texture, Form, and History. The reader may well be wondering at this stage how he is to deal with all of these matters, indeed whether he ought to. In what way should the four methods be combined? Well, in the first place, there is no absolutely imperative need that they should. It is better to teach one method thoroughly and with conviction than to attempt more than teacher and pupil can cope with. Having said this, I hasten to add that all four should be done if possible. In my opinion the order of importance is Form, Texture, Colour, History. In other words, if I have time only for three methods, then History is the first to go, and so on. But this is perhaps a personal preference. Anyone who feels strongly that the order is otherwise may please himself. The above, however, is not the best order in which the pupil should encounter these approaches. If the four *must* be taught one at a time, then the best order is probably Colour, Texture, Form, History. But I do not feel very strongly about this. What I do feel strongly about is that the four approaches should not be kept in watertight compartments. A little of one and then a little of another is a good thing. So the four approaches could run parallel from the earliest stages in a child's development. Here is a complete scheme I would recommend:

Age 5–7 (*Infants*)

Little or no formal teaching. Contact with short pieces of a tuneful and rhythmic nature, usually with a story or title which would capture the imagination. The best musical education at this age lies in singing, percussion band and other simple instrumental work, and music and movement.

Age 7–11 (*Juniors*)

Colour Any of schemes (1) to (4) in Chapter 2 (page 17).

Texture Types of Texture, and Listening to the Bass (see Chapter 3).

Form Theme counting, Rondo, Variations and Ternary form.

History Casual anecdotes about composers, etc., slipped in to accompany the playing of a piece. Perhaps a few set lessons on particular composers.

Age 11–14 (*Lower Seniors*)

Colour The Instruments of the Orchestra, Colour at work in music, and simple score reading.

Texture Schemes (2) to (6) (see Chapter 3).

Form Schemes (1) to (4) revised. Schemes (5) to (7) (see Chapter 4).

History Set lessons on a few famous composers.

Age 14–16 or more (*Upper Seniors*)

Colour Schemes (7) and (8). Any of schemes (1) (3) (5) and (6) at a more advanced level.

Texture Revision and expansion of previous schemes.

Form Sonata form, Deviations from Sonata form, and Sonata-Rondo form.

History All important composers, with lists of works. A more comprehensive History of Music for more advanced pupils.

Teachers might well consider working to the above scheme, particularly if they can feel that the previous stages have been carried out by other teachers responsible for their pupils' musical education. However, there are other ways of going about the whole matter. It should be possible to do good teaching by taking one piece of music at a time and teaching from one of the four aspects, according to the piece. For example, the teacher may decide one week to play the ballet music from *Rosamunde* and take the opportunity to talk about Schubert; the next lesson to use 'Jesu, joy of man's desiring' as an introduction to counterpoint; and the next lesson to use Khachaturyan's Lullaby from *Gayaneh* as a starting-point to talk about colour. This approach will suit the teacher who prefers not to be bound by a scheme. I hope its dangers are obvious: the teacher may drift, may leave lessons unprepared, and may fail to teach all that he ought. Yet another way is to introduce a piece at a time and treat it, more or less exhaustively, from all four angles. The danger here is of confusing the pupil with too many issues at once. However, a teacher with the right personality should pull it off. The pieces would have to be carefully chosen, and the lessons could not be short ones. It would suit a school where Musical Appreciation lessons are fairly rare, for whatever reason. Better would be to spread the study of the pieces over several lessons each.

It is more likely that a teacher who does adopt the non-schematic approach will be able to use, not necessarily either one or all four of the above main aspects, but one, two, three, or four according to the piece (and, of course, according to the readiness or otherwise of the pupils to receive them). Repeated hearings of pieces are always vital to any method. Here again the various aspects would be best considered separately, at each hearing.

OTHER APPROACHES

To examine a piece of music from the angles of colour, texture, form, and history (or style) does not exhaust the possibilities. Those which follow can either be used independently of the 'Big Four', or may be allowed to arise naturally as part of a lesson mainly devoted to one or more of them.

(1) *Rhythm*

This can be discussed at any stage. At the simpler levels pupils can be invited to discover the time signature of a piece or to indicate the ends of phrases by raising a hand. Clapping the rhythm of a melody they have been hearing is useful, too. Although these activities are, strictly speaking, in the nature of aural training, they are useful in directing the listener's attention to an aspect of music which may otherwise get overlooked. Young pupils should know that marches are in duple and waltzes in triple time. Later the pupil can add to his store of knowledge of such matters. For example, although waltzes, minuets, mazurkas, and polonaises are all in triple time, each has a characteristic rhythmic figure in the accompaniment which distinguishes it from other dances. Cross-rhythms and syncopations can be pointed out when the moment seems ripe. (It should not be overlooked that such things

are to be found in the music of all the great classical composers.) Older pupils and adults will encounter the complexities of quintuple time (e.g. Holst's *Mars*—don't forget
to compare the basic $\frac{5}{4}$ pattern with the twice-as-slow $\frac{5}{2}$ of
the middle section), irregular and unpredictable accents
(e.g. Adolescents' Dance in Stravinsky's *Rite of Spring*), and
rhythmic metamorphoses of themes (such as occur in
much of Walton's music, e.g. Viola Concerto). Phrasing is
an important aspect of rhythm and can be taught in
appropriate stages. Pupils should be taught to feel bars as
slow beats and feel the normality of the four-bar phrase
before going on to irregularities in phrase structure.

(2) *Melody*

This also can arise at any stage. Without necessarily
analysing the complete piece from a formal point of view,
various features of the melody can be pointed out. Much
depends on the actual melody, but such things as balancing
phrases, climax, and sequence can be taught to junior
schoolchildren. Sometimes in a song there is a particularly
apt expression of the words to be found in the melody. For
example, in Brahms's 'The Blacksmith' the leaps of the
vocal line suggest the swinging of the blacksmith's hammer
(to say nothing of the 'sparks' effect in the piano accompaniment). Of course, some of this work can be done in
the singing lesson. With older children attention can be
drawn to such hidden treasures as immediate melodic
development and varied repeats or inversions. At a higher
level still melody can occasionally be analysed in minute
detail. One useful way is to begin by playing only the first
phrase of a melody and inviting the class to suggest how it
should continue. Their suggestions are then compared with

the actual composition, presumably with edifying results. If this method is impracticable, the teacher himself can suggest an obvious or pedestrian continuation and go on to make a similar comparison. Other methods of presenting melodies will, one hopes, suggest themselves to the teacher. The precise method will depend on the melody itself and the teacher's understanding of it.

As an example of the sort of thing mentioned above, let us consider the St. Antony Chorale (as used by Haydn and Brahms). Junior pupils could be shown the sequences in the middle section, senior pupils the varied recapitulation and irregular phrasing, adults the reasons for the latter two, followed by a discussion on the relative merits of exact and inexact symmetry.

(3) *Programme Music*

It is, of course, false that all music represents something. You know this and I know this, but there is grave danger that children may come to believe this falsity. Programme music is often great fun and should be introduced from time to time. But let it be made clear that it is exceptional, a 'treat' if you like. Constantly guard against the giving of any impression that music *without* a picture or story is somehow inferior. (And also guard against any impression, perhaps in yourself, that the opposite is true: that programme music is inferior.) The truth is that a programme is in the last resort completely irrelevant—music must be enjoyed for its own sake: for its musical qualities. So, in presenting a piece of programme music, be careful not to admire it for the skill with which the composer carries out his job as illustrator, but to admire it for the sort of musical qualities we would look for in an abstract piece. If you do not agree with this, then you presumably rate Honegger's

Pacific 231 higher than Mendelssohn's *Fingal's Cave*, and the bleating sheep episode in Strauss's *Don Quixote* above the main 'Quixote' melody of the piece. It is interesting to reflect that in the visual arts of painting and sculpture, absolute realism is regarded not as a desirable quality but as a positive drawback: what matter are such things as line, colour, pattern, rhythm, design, feeling, and so on. And this in a field where the vast majority of works purport to represent something!

At some stage in the pupil's life this matter could be brought into the open and the phrases Programme Music and Absolute (or Abstract) Music introduced. Older pupils and adults might enjoy a discussion involving the principles given above. In the meantime, let us all enjoy ourselves with our small but legitimate ration of programme music. Some well-tried suggestions follow:

For young pupils:

Rimsky-Korsakov: *Flight of the Bumble Bee*
Prokofiev: *Peter and the Wolf*
Saint-Saëns: *Carnival of the Animals*

For 11–14s:

Arnold: *Tam O' Shanter*
Dukas: *The Sorcerer's Apprentice*
Mendelssohn: *Fingal's Cave*
 Midsummer Night's Dream, Overture
Mussorgsky: *Night on a Bare Mountain*
Smetana: *Vltava*
Wagner: *Ride of the Valkyries*

For older pupils:

Beethoven: *Pastoral Symphony*
Berlioz: *Fantastic Symphony*

Debussy: *Prélude à l'après-midi d'un faune*
Honegger: *Pacific 231*
Mussorgsky: *Pictures at an Exhibition*
Sibelius: *Swan of Tuonela*
  Tapiola
  Oceanides
Strauss: *Till Eulenspiegel*
  Don Quixote

Akin to Programme Music is Characteristic Music, which, although having no detailed story or scene, has a particular character indicated by the title. Together with theatre and ballet music, and, of course, all vocal music, we have countless pieces associated with extra-musical ideas in varying degrees from near-abstract to near-programme. A few examples will show the sort of thing:

Schumann: *Album for the Young*
  Scenes from Childhood
Tchaikovsky: *Nutcracker* Suite
  Swan Lake
Bizet: *Carmen* Suite
Grieg: *Peer Gynt* Incidental Music
Stravinsky: *Firebird*
  Petrushka

(4) *Miscellaneous Methods*

(a) *BBC broadcasts*

Regularly listening to, or watching one of the BBC'S schools programmes is one way of solving the teacher's problems. Many of the courses are excellent. Even those who prefer to handle things themselves might consider slipping an odd broadcast in now and then. Again, if the time happens to be right, a broadcast concert could be

used. It at least sets a good example that some of the pupils
might learn to follow for themselves.

(b) Score reading

This has been referred to before. It is a most valuable
aid to teaching Musical Appreciation. But it has its
dangers: (i) the teacher may think pupils are getting
benefits they are not, e.g. they may not be able to read
music well enough to follow and may waste time looking
for the place, or they may read only the melody line
although the teacher thinks they follow everything; (ii) the
teacher may rely too much on score reading as an end in
itself (or as a means of keeping the class quiet) and fail to
teach other aspects of music. But, provided the teacher is
careful to be sympathetic and helpful about the mechanics
of score reading, especially in the early stages; and provided he uses scores as an *aid* to teaching, much benefit can
be gained by the class. Colour and texture are almost automatically dealt with at all stages, and it is easy to teach
form with the scores in front of the pupils. Again I recommend Fiske's *Score Reading* (four books, Oxford University
Press) as a ready-made scheme. Another useful book is
Long's *Listening to Music in Secondary Schools* (Boosey &
Hawkes). Both of these publications put all the necessary
material into the pupils' hands. Sets of miniature scores
might also gradually be acquired. In the case of choral
works such as *Messiah* it is perhaps possible to borrow a set
of vocal scores from a local organist or choral society for
use in this way.

(c) Symbolic notation

Where scores are impracticable I have often made use
of symbols invented on the spur of the moment. I put these

on the board to represent themes, and can often plot out a complete piece in diagrammatic form. If I am concentrating on the appearances of one main theme only and regarding all others as subsidiary, a straight line will do, with wiggles or dots for the unimportant parts. For example, here is the opening of Fugue No. 2 from Bach's '48':

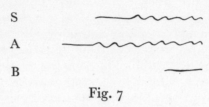

S

A

B

Fig. 7

To show the pitch aspect of a theme, I go up and down; thus the horn theme beginning the second subject of Beethoven's Fifth Symphony, 1st movement, could appear thus:

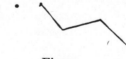

Fig. 8

Or the *motion* of the theme could be shown more graphically thus:

Fig. 9

The first half of the Minuet of Mozart's Symphony No. 40 comes out like this:

Fig. 10

But to make such metaphors meaningful to the class it is best to sing the theme while actually writing it up, so that they see how the 'notation' works. The whole thing must not be allowed to become too complicated or it will defeat its purpose, which is *clarity*. And remember it is only done so as to illustrate some point or make a theme more memorable.

(d) Playing pieces without comment

If not overdone, this is harmless enough as an occasional practice in the music lesson. A particularly useful opportunity to do this may occur as pupils assemble for the morning service. The music must be suitable, of course, though this does not mean everything must be solemn or religious. Classical symphonies, concertos, and suites, for example, offer many possibilities. As the children leave the hall, another, brighter piece will give them a 'lift' and even send them humming to their first lesson. This has become common practice in many schools. The titles of the music, plus any further details of composer, etc., the teacher may think fit, are placed where interested pupils may find them. Even the uninterested pupils are being subliminally educated by this means. Let each pair of pieces be played for a week to achieve the necessary repetition.

(e) Letting pupils bring records

Now and then the class could be invited to bring their

favourite records. The teacher should do this with his eyes open, and be prepared for some undesirable pieces to turn up! So only do this if you're prepared to take the rough with the smooth. See next chapter for further comments on this practice ('Meeting the pupil half-way').

(*f*) *Playing request items*

Done occasionally, this will give the teacher a valuable guide to the way his pupils' tastes are forming. It will also give the pupils pleasure. But it should not be done too often; the teacher must never sink to the degrading position of disc jockey.

(*g*) *Organising trips to concerts, etc.*

The value of this is obvious and it should be done whenever possible. It's a little extra work for the teacher, who, of course, must go along himself. This kind of thing should not be confined to visits to concerts by professional orchestras, but should extend to solo recitals and perfor- mances by local choral or operatic societies (*if* the music is worth while), and even to performances by other schools in the area. This aspect of Musical Appreciation is most important. We must all maintain contact with live music and not come to rely entirely upon recorded sounds. It is particularly valuable to study a piece in class and then to hear it at a live concert.

(5) *Bad or dangerous approaches*

The first two of these at least are common enough to deserve a special word of warning: namely that they appear plausible until one looks hard at them. I fear, however, that teachers will continue to be found who believe tenaciously in these methods.

(a) *Appealing to the pupils' imagination*

The method is to select a piece of programme music,
play it without giving the title, and invite the pupils to
supply a title or detailed interpretation, either verbally or
on paper. A very little experience of this ought to convince
any teacher that he can hope for no sort of accuracy in the
results. Even if he should get it, he has nothing to con-
gratulate himself or his pupils on. To return once more to
the analogy of painting, let us imagine a lesson in which
the teacher shows his class one picture after another and
asks what they represent. 'Please, sir, a portrait of a lady.'
'Yes, good; and this one?' 'It's a wagon of hay in a puddle
near a farmhouse.' 'Excellent' . . . and so on. Can anyone seriously think that this would be a lesson on Art
Appreciation? The fact that in music it is *harder* to do
this should not blind us to the fact that the same argument
applies. Appreciating music means appreciating music.

Even worse is the practice of playing abstract music and
asking for the same sort of thing. No further reason need be
given: the above argument applies with even more force.
Yet (it may be argued) if the listener really is stimulated
by the music to imagine so-and-so, what is the harm in
talking about it, if he is really honest? There are all sorts
of reasons why not, but one will do for the moment:
because the time could be better spent otherwise. Believe me, I've
given this method a fair trial, and regret every minute
wasted on it. To hear such imaginative fantasies as descriptions of 'running through trees with somebody after
me' (a fairly popular one with boys in connexion with all
sorts of music) may throw a little light on the Freudian
fears inhabiting some youngsters' minds; or to read silly
girls' romantic descriptions of moonlight and waterfalls

may tell us something about the writers; but what are *we* doing for the *pupils*? Stimulating their imaginations, you may reply. More's the pity if that's what they come up with, is my rejoinder. But more of this later.

(b) Asking pupils for their emotional response

Whether the piece be abstract or programme music, the pupils are asked how they feel, or what feelings the music arouses, or what feelings the music expresses, and so on. This process *may* be quite valuable, but it depends how it is done. Sooner or later the pupil must acknowledge the fact that music is concerned with the emotions, but let the teacher beware of the difficulties involved. In the first place it is unwise to dwell too long on this aspect of listening to music. If the teacher is constantly making an issue out of it, the pupil who has little or no emotional reaction (and this may be perfectly proper) may either dishonestly profess to non-existent feelings or worry himself into imagining unnatural ones. Or again he may lose patience with the whole subject! I would be very wary of asking a pupil how he feels. The reason is that there is nothing useful to be done with his answer. Supposing he says, 'The music makes me feel happy' when he has just heard *Eine Kleine Nachtmusik*, do we praise him and tell him he's quite right; or if he says it makes him feel sad, do we tell him he's wrong? Surely teaching Musical Appreciation does not consist of telling people how they should feel, for if they have the 'wrong' feelings, nothing can be done about it. Rather less reprehensible would be to ask *what feelings the composer is trying to express*. Here if the answer is 'wrong' we might go on to say 'That's interesting. What makes you think so?' and make a gentle attempt to convince the pupil that a different interpretation might be more true. Thus

again, if he says of *Eine Kleine Nachtmusik* that Mozart is
expressing sadness by his energetic tunes, he could be
reminded that tunes of this type are generally agreed to
express joy. (Whereas, may I repeat, if the pupil says that
he himself *feels* sadness as a result of the music, no argument is possible.) However, I must admit that we are not
much better off, even with this revised form of the question,
if we get a difficult pupil.

In other words, to raise the whole matter is to court
trouble. It should be directly alluded to as little as possible.
Remembering the value of infectious enthusiasm on our
part, and using our 'diffident confidence', we may from
time to time refer to this 'gay tune' or that 'sinister passage'
or this 'amusing piece'. Especially if such remarks are
casually dropped *before* playing the music, the pupils will
probably respond to our suggestions and think upon our
lines. In case any reader should at this stage be thinking
that this attitude is unwarrantably presumptuous, I must
refer him back to Chapter 1, and ask him to consider the
chaotic alternative that will ensue if he allows himself to
believe that his pupils' opinions are as good as his. The
pupils are not as familiar with music as we are. *It is our job
to teach them.* But keep the 'emotional expression' angle in
its proper place, which is subsidiary to the main task of
teaching *understanding*.

(c) Overdoing the 'infectious enthusiasm'

Always to say to the class, as you play them your
favourite pieces, 'Listen to this, it's beautiful', or 'This is
great music', or (at the end) 'That was good, wasn't it?'
and such remarks, can be dangerous. If you constantly do
this you may make a spectacle of yourself and get derisive
sniggers from your class—especially if that's *all* you do.

Enthusiastic praise is no substitute for teaching. But as a minor *supplement* to more helpful teaching it has definite value.

(d) Overdoing analysis

Taking a piece of music apart is fine if it helps us to understand it better. But let's not forget to put the bits together again. Analysis should always be followed by a complete run-through of a piece, so that the whole can be grasped.

But, of course, overdoing anything is dangerous. Even teaching!

(e) Choosing examples only from the teacher's favourite pieces

This is not so much a method of teaching as a danger inherent in any method. Most of us have 'blind spots' for particular composers or pieces. It is only too easy to keep such things from our pupils, who, needless to say, are not obliged to share our prejudices. In saying this I am not pleading for an undiscriminating use of wheat and chaff alike. The teacher *must* use his influence to bring his pupils into contact with the best music. But a composer who is disliked by the teacher must not be excluded if the rest of the world rates him highly. Although the teacher will not be able to show genuine enthusiasm, he can at least see that his pupils have a chance to do so. Thus I personally dislike Schubert, but I let my pupils hear his music. I try not to bring about a situation where my dislike is called into question: I will use his songs to illustrate figurative accompaniment, or his symphonies to show form, or his *Rosamunde* music to show orchestration. In other words, I find some aspect I can be objective about. I fancy many teachers dislike modern music, but it is their duty to put a reasonable share of it before their pupils, without making disparaging remarks or implying disparagement in any way—the supercilious smile, the lifted eyebrow, etc.

PLANNING A SYLLABUS

Please do work to a syllabus. Although I have stressed the freedom of individual approach which the teacher should exercise, I must add that it takes a very old hand to 'play it by ear' successfully. Having decided which lines of attack you prefer, plan the work out logically so that pieces of music will illustrate points progressively and not haphazardly. Put it down on paper and stick to it until experience proves you wrong. I would go further and recommend teachers to prepare notes on individual lessons. Arrange them in a loose-leaf file so that failures can be removed and replaced, or the order altered if experience so dictates.

Include in your scheme plenty of revision, and see that pieces of music get repeated hearings, either within the lesson or spread over several lessons. In the latter case pieces can either come up again to serve a new purpose or can be repeated as part of a no-comment listen-for-pleasure part of the lesson. But don't make a fetish of repeating absolutely every piece.

Relate your scheme as far as possible to all other musical activities in the school, both in the choice of pieces and in methods of cross-relationships with singing, aural training, etc. As to the amount of time spent on the subject, perhaps only the individual can decide, but it is worth remembering two points: (1) Few children, however hard we try, will pursue active music-making when they leave school. (2) But they will all presumably have radio and television of their own at some future time, and the exercise of discretion in visiting concerts, etc. We can justify every minute spent on teaching Musical Appreciation if it will mean that they will listen to good music and visit worthwhile concerts. A regular proportion of time, say a quarter to a half of total music teaching time, devoted to acquiring a technique of listening to music is necessary to achieve this aim.

CHOOSING MUSIC

Having decided on his method of attack, the teacher must equip himself with an adequate supply of pieces. The requirements for these are:

(1) *They should be appropriate to the pupil.* This does not imply that the pupil must always be able to understand *everything* in a piece (do you?), but he must be able to find a good deal which he can grasp.

(2) *They should stimulate the pupil in some way.* This is linked with the above point. Listening to music should involve the pupil in both a familiar and a challenging activity: it should be within his grasp if he stretches a little. He may dimly sense beauty, he may crudely feel drama, he may partly understand logic: this is all good, if there still remains something for him to work at.

(3) *They should cover everything.* Between them, the pieces will show (as far as may be possible) all kinds of media, vocal and instrumental, orchestral, chamber, and solo music; and all periods and composers.

It should be apparent that some of the examples played to the class ought to be piano solos played by the teacher (if he can be sure to put up a reasonable performance). This fulfils the condition of providing live music, and such performances are usually followed with an interest not given to recording. None the less the majority of the music played will be recorded. The number of records needed to deal with the subject is quite large, and the question arises where they are to come from. Ideally they are all in stock as the property of the school. In practice the teacher will probably use some of his own personal records, regrettable though this may be. Many local authorities have a central library of records available on loan to schools. This system has the drawbacks (*a*) that one cannot rely on having a piece just when one wants it, and (*b*) that records often arrive in a worn or damaged condition. All the same a central library has undeniable advantages (particularly if it is, as it should be, quite large and contains out-of-the-way pieces including the whole of the *History of Music in Sound*), and teachers in areas where such facilities are not available should consider getting their heads together and requesting them. As to the school stock of records, it will just have to be built up year by year as funds afford. But do guard your collection carefully. My advice is to let *no one* but yourself use it—don't lend records to the P.E. staff for dancing, etc. They should have their own records and record-player. This may seem mean, but music is your stock in trade and your precious records should be preserved from any possible harm.

To assist teachers in building up a stock of records there follow suggestions for basic collections. It is emphasised that these will be supplemented by records representing the teacher's personal preferences. It is also emphasised that the playing of piano pieces will supplement the lists. Many suggestions for these have already been made, but the final choice will depend on the skill of the teacher as a performer, and on his stock of music.

(1) *A basic minimum collection for junior schools*

Chopin: *Les Sylphides*

Clarke: Trumpet Voluntary
Delibes: *Coppelia* Ballet Suite
Grieg: *Peer Gynt* Suite No. 1
Handel: *Water Music*
Mozart: *Eine Kleine Nachtmusik*
Prokofiev: *Peter and the Wolf*
Saint-Saëns: *Carnival of the Animals*
Tchaikovsky: *Nutcracker* Suite

(2) *Additional suggestions for junior schools*

Bach: Air and Gavotte from Suite No. 3 for orchestra
 'Jesu, joy of man's desiring'
Britten: *The Young Person's Guide to the Orchestra*
Chabrier: *España*
Debussy: *Children's Corner* Suite
Delibes: *Sylvia* Ballet Suite
Dukas: *The Sorcerer's Apprentice*
Dvořák: Slavonic Dances
Elgar: *Pomp and Circumstance Marches 1 and 4*
 Three Bavarian Dances
 Wand of Youth
Grieg: Norwegian Dances
Handel: *Messiah* (extracts)
Kodály: *Háry János* Suite
Prokofiev: *Love of Three Oranges* Suite
 Lieutenant Kije
Quilter: *Children's Overture*
Ravel: *Mother Goose* Suite
Schubert: *Rosamunde* Ballet
Strauss: *Radetzky March*
Strauss: *Blue Danube*
 Tales from the Vienna Woods
Tchaikovsky: *Swan Lake* Ballet Suite
Vaughan Williams: *English Folk Songs* Suite
 Fantasia on Greensleeves

Warlock: *Capriol* Suite
As many solo recitals as desired (see list 4)

(3) *A basic minimum collection for senior schools*

All, if possible, of the above, plus:

Bach: Suite No. 2, for orchestra
Beethoven: *Egmont* Overture
    Symphony No. 5
Berlioz: *Hungarian March*, from *Damnation of Faust*
    Roman Carnival Overture
Bizet: *L'Arlésienne* Suites 1 and 2
    Carmen Suite
Brahms: St. Antony Variations
Dvořák: 'New World' Symphony
Elgar: 'Enigma' Variations
Haydn: Symphony No. 101 ('Clock')
Holst: *The Planets*
Mendelssohn: *Hebrides* Overture
    Midsummer Night's Dream Overture, etc.
Mozart: Symphony No. 40
    Horn Concerto No. 4
    Marriage of Figaro Overture
Schubert: Unfinished Symphony
Sibelius: *Karelia* Suite
Stravinsky: *Firebird* Suite
Tchaikovsky: Symphony No. 4
Wagner: *Ride of the Valkyries*

(4) *Additional suggestions for senior schools*

Bach: Brandenburg Concertos 2, 3, 4, 5
    Suites 1, 3, 4, for orchestra
    Violin Concerto in E
    Concerto for two violins
    Fantasia and Fugue in G minor, for organ
    Passacaglia and Fugue in C minor, for organ
    Cantata No. 140, 'Wachet Auf'

Bartók: Concerto for orchestra
  Music for Strings, Percussion and Celesta
Beethoven: Symphonies 3, 6, 7
  'Emperor' Concerto
  Violin Concerto
  Overture, *Leonora No. 3*
  String Quartet Op. 59, No. 1
  String Quartet Op. 131
  'Archduke' Trio
Berg: *Wozzeck* (extracts)
Berlioz: *Fantastic Symphony*
Borodin: *Polovtsian Dances*
Brahms: Symphony No. 4
  Violin Concerto
Britten: *Serenade*
  Four Sea Interludes from *Peter Grimes*
Chopin: Polonaise in A
  Polonaise in A♭
  Fantaisie-Impromptu
Debussy: *Prélude à l'après-midi d'un faune*
  La Mer
  Nocturnes
Delius: *Brigg Fair*
  On hearing the first cuckoo in Spring
Dohnanyi: *Variations on a nursery theme*
Dvořák: Cello Concerto
Falla: *El Amor Brujo*, Ballet
Fauré: *Pavane*
Franck: Symphonic Variations
  Violin Sonata
Grieg: Piano Concerto
Haydn: Symphonies 100 and 104
  Trumpet Concerto (finale)
  Creation (extracts)
Khachaturyan: *Gayaneh* Ballet
Liszt: Hungarian Rhapsody No. 15 (Rakoczy March)

Mendelssohn: Violin Concerto
  'Italian' Symphony
Mozart: Symphonies 29, 39, 41
  Clarinet Quintet
  Piano Concerto in A, K. 488
  String Quartet in C, K. 465
  Marriage of Figaro (extracts)
  Magic Flute (extracts)
  Don Giovanni (extracts)
Mussorgsky: *Night on a Bare Mountain*
  Pictures at an Exhibition
Purcell: *Dido and Aeneas*
Rachmaninov: *Rhapsody on a theme of Paganini*
Ravel: *Bolero*
  La Valse
Rimsky-Korsakov: *Capriccio Espagnol*
  Scheherazade
Schubert: Octet
  String Quartet in A minor
  Lieder: 'Erlking', '2 Grenadiers', etc.
Schumann: Piano Concerto
Sibelius: Symphony No. 2
  Swan of Tuonela
  Tapiola
Smetana: *Bartered Bride* Overture
Strauss: *Don Quixote*
  Till Eulenspiegel
Stravinsky: *Petrushka*
  Rite of Spring
  The Soldier's Tale
  Symphony of Psalms
Tchaikovsky: Symphonies 5 and 6
  Piano Concerto No. 1
  Violin Concerto
  Romeo and Juliet
Tippett: *Ritual Dances* from *Midsummer Marriage*

Vaughan Williams: *Fantasia on a theme of Thomas Tallis*
 Sinfonia Antartica
Verdi: *Rigoletto* (excerpts)
 Aida (excerpts)
Wagner: *Mastersingers* Overture
 Mastersingers (extracts)
 Tristan and Isolde Prelude
 Tannhaüser Overture
Walton: *Façade* Suites 1 and 2
 Two Pieces for Strings (*Henry V*)
 Belshazzar's Feast
Weber: *Oberon* Overture
 Der Freischütz Overture

Solo recitals by:

Joan Sutherland (soprano)
Janet Baker (contralto)
Peter Pears (tenor)
Owen Brannigan (bass)
Dietrich Fischer-Dieskau (baritone)
Gyorgy Cziffra (piano)
Jascha Heifetz (violin)
Mstislav Rostropovich (cello)
Leon Goossens (oboe)
Thurston Dart (organ, clavichord and harpsichord)
Julian Bream (guitar and lute)

Any further requirements for teaching History of Music
are best taken from *History of Music in Sound*, a collection
so comprehensive that individual teachers will select from
it according to their special interests. Even without it, the
above list may well seem so huge as to appear totally
beyond the bounds of possibility. But put together in the
order given, it can be slowly built up over several years.
Is it all necessary? Yes and no: a good teacher can put

the subject across successfully with surprisingly few pieces; on the other hand, there is enormous value in having to hand a piece to illustrate a particular point as it arises. Although any one pupil would probably not hear every piece on the list even were they in stock, I doubt very much whether any record would gather dust in a grammar school with a vigorous music teacher, especially if he runs an out-of-school gramophone club.

7. In the Classroom

It is not for me to show the reader how normal classroom discipline is maintained. He has this ability already or he has it not. But it sometimes happens that a teacher who has no trouble with his singing lessons finds that in his Musical Appreciation lessons the discipline is harder to maintain; or if discipline be good, maybe there are signs of unrest or lack of interest. What is wrong and how can it be cured? First, the lesson may lack interest because the teacher is an uninteresting teacher: he lacks the fortunate ability to 'put things across' in a fascinating manner. This does not matter quite so much in a singing lesson where the pupils have plenty to keep them occupied, but it could show up in the same teacher's Appreciation lesson, if the pupils are taking a passive role. Second, the teacher may lack confidence in his ability to deal with the subject, and this may show in his teaching. In both cases the only remedies are constant heart-searching and efforts at self-improvement by the teacher. This is his affair, and detailed help from me is quite outside the scope of this book. Third, the teacher may be using one of the bad methods outlined in the previous chapter. The class may be interested for a while, but will soon become restive because they can sense that they are not learning anything. Fourth, the pupils may be uninterested because they have not been given anything to do (or think they have not, which comes to the same thing).

Now, this last reason I find to be the most common error in the teaching of the subject. It is not enough that we have said 'Listen to this music'. This is not definite enough, it is too *huge* a task and the pupil can easily get discouraged because the Promised Land does not immediately fling wide its gates. Give him something to listen *for*, some definite task, and (most important of all) *something which lies within his power to do*. Nothing succeeds like success, and nothing deters like constant failure. If your pupils are continually being given jobs which they can succeed at, they will be interested and discipline will never be a problem.

Another necessary condition of maintaining discipline and interest is that the teacher himself must appear interested. The class can hardly be expected to concentrate if there is no good example coming from the teacher. He must learn the art of apparently listening with downcast gaze and rapt attention to the music whilst he keeps a surreptitious eye on his class to be sure that all is well. If someone does misbehave, he will get a direct stare and be dealt with afterwards. Strolling round the room is distracting and should not be necessary. Worse than strolling is to sit marking books or doing some similar task. And, believe it or not, I knew a teacher whose habit was to start the record-player and then *leave the room*! For what purpose I never did discover, but there the pupils were, there the record was—and the result can be imagined. No wonder when another teacher took over that some of the class beseeched: '*Please* don't play us any records.'

THE PUPIL'S TASK

The pupil, then, should whenever possible be given a

definite task—something to listen *for*. The obvious corollary of this is that he should be tested somehow to see if he has heard it. Try to make it a normal part of the lesson to expect a contribution, verbal or written, from the class. Let us deal with the possible verbal contributions first.

At the lowest level the class may be asked such simple questions as 'Was the speed fast or slow?' 'Was it loud or soft, or did it change from one to the other?' 'What instruments took part?' Certain other obvious and verifiable facts can be asked for; for example, in listening to a Rondo or Ground Bass we may ask how many times the main theme was heard, whether it was varied, which instrument played it and so on. Or the class may raise hands when a theme returns. In a Texture lesson, the pupils could be asked what type of texture is used (theme in bass, harmonic accompaniment, two-part counterpoint, fugue, etc.). Naming prominent solo instruments could be asked for, and even, with older children, naming accompanying instruments. In variations pupils could be asked what has happened to the tune. It is important to realise that we normally give notice of all these questions by saying what they are going to be *before* the music is played. Let me repeat my solemn warning against asking the pupils what the music means, or represents; or asking them how the music makes them feel. I do not wish to forbid such things *entirely*; an occasional question on those lines may be thrown in along with the more factual business, but the matter should never be allowed to loom large in the minds of the pupils. And again I repeat that it is less reprehensible to ask what mood they think the composer is trying to express (or what the character of the music is).

Considering all these possible approaches together, it

may be said that what we are aiming at is the gradual
cultivation of the pupil's ability to describe accurately the
music he hears and to give it some sort of evaluation. In a
word, to appreciate. I personally expect older pupils to be
able to do this with a fair degree of observation and judge-
ment. One hopes that, as adults, these same pupils will
have learnt never to argue about artistic matters without
backing up their opinions with supporting facts. How
pleased I was the other day when I got the first glimmer-
ings of this attitude from a student. For months she had
been a passive member of her group. She had contributed
nothing to discussions and apparently gained nothing from
them.

I was talking to the group about repetition as the basis
of musical form, and we had made merry at the amount of
over-repetition we found in a certain pop record. Afterwards, playing a record of Handel's 'O ruddier than the
cherry' from *Acis and Galatea* as an example of Da Capo
form, I got, at long last, a reaction and a verbal contribution from this young lady. 'Everybody was laughing at
the repetitions in the pop record,' she said indignantly, 'but
I thought the Handel piece had far more repetition—it
was ridiculous.' I think she was rather surprised when I
expressed great pleasure at her statement. I let her see that
her expression of dislike was worth examining because it
was backed up by facts. (Actually she got her facts wrong
on this occasion, for the Handel was *not* more repetitious
than the pop record, but to dash cold water on the student
at this crucial stage would do her no good. Flushed with
success at her 'defeat' of me, she will in future, I feel sure,
search eagerly for more facts in support of her opinions of
music.) What emerges from this tale is the importance of
not condemning outright any attempts by our pupils to

pass judgements which are genuinely and properly felt. Give all opinions sympathetic consideration and ask the person concerned to explain his attitude with reference to what is going on in the music. (If he cannot do this, we still have much to teach him.) It is only silly and ill-considered opinions that need reprimanding.

Turning now to written work, I must begin by warning the teacher not to let it occupy too much time from the normal lesson. Written work can be of four kinds:

(1) *Note-taking*

Notes dictated by the teacher will summarise his most important lessons in a form easily used for later revision by the pupils. They should be as brief as possible.

(2) *Record of pieces heard*

The pupil's notebook could have a section (say at the back) where he keeps a record of all the pieces he hears, in three columns: date, composer, title. This need take only a few seconds from a lesson. What does it achieve? Perhaps very little, except to impress a title deeper on the memory (writing anything down does this) and to provide a permanent record for revision purposes. By all means omit it if you feel it is not worth the trouble.

(3) *Tests*

Now and then a test or quiz (call it what you will) is a good idea. This can include questions on facts taught by the teacher (that is to say non-musical facts such as that a French horn is made of brass, or Bach had twenty children, or Elgar wrote the 'Enigma' Variations); or better still, listening tests in which short extracts of records are played (or reproduced on the piano) for identification; or best of all, listening tests which ask the pupil to make a specific musical discovery for himself. For suggestions, see above, where verbal work was discussed.

(4) *Descriptions of pieces*

A lengthier job is the writing of a composition by the pupil describing a piece of music. This can take various forms:

(*a*) *A factual description*, as accurate as possible, to test the pupil's observation. The criterion here is that an experienced musician reading the description should be able to identify the piece without being told the title! Descriptive or emotive adjectives are completely avoided. Here is an example of the kind of thing:

'At the beginning, cellos and basses play very low down, quietly, with no other instruments playing. The melody rises a little and immediately falls lower and lower. This only takes a few bars, then violins join in with a kind of simple tune in which they seem to play every note twice in rapid succession; meanwhile the cellos pluck. When this has been done twice a tune is added on the woodwind. It begins by a two-note drop followed by a few more notes, then this is repeated.'

Does the reader recognise this as the beginning of Schubert's Unfinished Symphony? Well, I did my best. Children will not manage as well as this normally, so be tolerant.

(*b*) *A subjective description* of the effects produced on the listener. For example:

'The beginning was brooding and mysterious—I felt that something was threatening me. Then a sort of shivering came into the music, and immediately a wailing tune was heard, like the voice of doom.'

Again this was the Unfinished Symphony.

(c) *A compromise* between the two foregoing methods. The attentive reader will have realised that they lie perilously near two arid extremes which have already been condemned in this book. One is too factual and unimaginative, the other is too vague and fanciful. It seems to me that an intelligent compromise represents a reasonable attitude to descriptive appreciation. So a better result than either of the foregoing examples would be:

'Cellos and basses begin by playing, unaccompanied, a brooding melody low down. A few bars later the violins begin a shivering accompaniment and the cellos pluck beneath them. Over this the woodwind then play a wailing theme.'

I like this approach, because any subjective reactions are linked with a specific cause in the music. Normally this kind of work can only be produced by carefully trained listeners with a reasonable command of English, in other words older pupils. There is no reason, though, why younger children should not occasionally try it, provided due allowances are made. At whatever stage, the teacher should encourage the production of the third kind of example given above. Remember that this involves *both* a factual *and* a subjective approach, so that exercises on the first two methods, regrettable though they are as ends in themselves, may be needed as a preparation. In any case, don't expect too long a piece of work. Set either a detailed description of a short passage, or a looser description of a whole piece, and set this kind of task only occasionally.

THE ACTUAL LESSON

Much has been said about all the various lines a teacher should or should not take. Now it is time to consider how the teacher is occupied during a single lesson. If only this were a straightforward task! But, as I have said in Chapter 1, so much depends on the music, on the pupil, and, most of all, on the teacher. For example, the piano is useful in illustrating all kinds of points and should be employed constantly to clarify the music under consideration, but only if the teacher is facile enough at the keyboard to make this worth while: otherwise he will have to sing to make his points, or use the record itself.

The most important involvement of the teacher's individuality and skill concerns how he occupies himself during a lesson. He will find himself involved in one or more of the following activities:

(1) Teaching hard facts
(2) Presenting a piece for appreciation, with some sort of descriptive analysis
(3) Testing the pupils' knowledge or perception
(4) Probing for pupils' reactions about mood, feeling, etc.
(5) Playing without comment or guidance
(6) Explaining the composer's intentions
(7) Showing enthusiasm

I would like the reader to consider these seven activities carefully. First, from the angle of what is informative, uncontroversial and educative in the factual sense, we have (1) and (2) as the only safe activities. Second, from the angle of what is inspiring and interesting though perhaps dangerous, we have (6) and (7). Third, we have (3) (4) and (5) which are more neutral, negative even. All these appear above in a rough progression from one extreme view to the other. Think of these extremes as representing two desirable peaks of attainment, with a trough between. The left-hand peak is somewhat higher than the right.

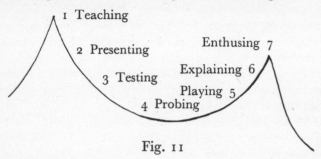

Fig. 11

Then *ideally* the teacher spends most time at the two peaks, flitting from one to the other. Don't carry the analogy too far: it is not necessary to traverse the gully every time one wishes to cross to the other peak! He will, however, spend *some* time on the lower reaches; least of all at the bottom. Very often all seven activities can occur in one and the same lesson; if not, *ideally* they occur in various lessons, in their proper proportions, spread over a longer period of time. *But*—and here's where the teacher's personality and individual experience are involved—he may find he teaches better through one particular activity, or that he does better on one side of the gully than on the other. Then I feel that his bias should be allowed to develop, provided that it is only a bias of emphasis. There should not be gaping holes in the diagram! (Although if there's one activity that might be spared, it is No. 4.)

And so there is no such thing as a typical lesson. Certain patterns will tend to repeat themselves, but nothing like a set routine should emerge. Sometimes a lesson may begin with revision, sometimes with the playing of a piece without comment, sometimes by the playing of a single theme and the building up of a complete piece from it, sometimes by showing a picture, and so on. All the same, I'll go so far as to provide the reader here with a specimen lesson. It happens to be a rather factual, down-to-earth lesson (because of its subject), but it will serve to show how the teacher moves between the seven activities, although some of them are barely touched on. It will also serve to show that the teacher does not allow either talking or music to go on for too long without switching from one to the other, and finally that he tries to avoid a lesson which uses only one piece of music.

A SPECIMEN LESSON ON MINUET AND TRIO FORM

(*The class imagined is 12–13 years old, in the middle stream of a mixed comprehensive school. Length of lesson, 30 minutes.*)

Good morning. Everybody ready? Just listen to this piece and put up your hand if you can tell me where you've heard it before.

(*Teacher starts record of Minuet from Mozart's 'Haffner' Symphony. After a few seconds a forest of hands shoots up. Teacher fades out record and selects a pupil to answer.*)

Please, sir, it's the piece we've had at Assembly all week.

(*The forest withers disappointedly.*)

Right, good. Now who can tell me what it's called?

(*This is a different matter. One hesitant hand rises.*)

I see you haven't been looking at the notice board!

(*You can't blame them. Whilst a good piece, this minuet is hardly full of the magic which makes children seethe with curiosity to know more about it. It was played at Assembly mainly as a preparation for this lesson.*)

Never mind. Well, Smith, can you tell us?

Was it a Mozart Symphony, sir?

Yes, it was. Well done. The 'Haffner' Symphony.

(*Teacher writes 'Haffner' swiftly on the board.*)

This particular part of the symphony was a dance. Can anyone tell me the name of a dance that was very popular when Mozart lived—the eighteenth century?

Please, sir, the Gavotte?

Quite true, that was an eighteenth-century dance. But this one was even more popular—the Minuet. You can tell the difference, because Gavottes always have four quick beats to a bar, and Minuets always have three. Listen.

(*Opening bars are played again.*)

Come on, count with me. *One*, two, three, *one*, two, three . . . All right!

(*Record is stopped.*)

Now I'd like you to see if you can find out what form this piece is in. I'll help you a bit. Here's the first section.

(*Teacher plays first 8 bars.*)

Here's the second.

(*Teacher plays next 8 bars, ignoring repeats.*)

And here's the next.

(*Teacher plays final 8 bars of the Minuet.*)

What did you notice about those three bits?

(*Many hands rise and teacher collects several answers. Class have recently learnt Ternary and Rondo form.*)

Please, sir, the first and third were the same. It was ABA, sir. Please, sir, was it Ternary? etc.

Very good. What you heard was in three parts, ABA, which we call Ternary. I'll put the bits together now. But there's one more thing. Do you remember how Ternary pieces often have repeats?

(*Writes on board:* A :‖: B A :‖)

And how that comes out like this?

(*Writes:* A A B A B A)

Try not to get muddled. Cross off the repeats in your mind. Say to yourself 'It's only a repeat; it doesn't count.' Now here we go.

(*Teacher plays Minuet with repeats, calling out at the appropriate times 'A', 'A repeat', 'B', 'A', 'B repeat', 'A again'.*)

All right, everybody?

(*Class appears happy about this point. Just as well, otherwise the teacher would have gone no further with the lesson until they were. But this is all, so far, revision of the lesson on Ternary form.*)

One more thing, before we go on. Why did musicians have these repeats?

To make the piece longer, sir.

Yes. Any other reason? . . . Well, it gives the listener a second chance to learn the tune, doesn't it, so he can remember it better and recognise it when it comes later. He can understand the piece better if he hears it twice. Now I'll give you some more music to analyse.

Please, sir, what's analyse?

It means to break up, see what a thing's made of. We've just done it once, haven't we? Then you can tell me what form this music is in. Look out for repeats.

(*Teacher plays Trio of 'Haffner' Symphony, with repeats, and gets the answer Ternary.*)

Well done. And did you notice this was a minuet also?

(*The class nod hypocritically. They didn't notice, because they were too busy analysing the form; and the teacher knows this, but he also knows when not to waste time.*)

As a matter of fact, it belongs with the other minuet we heard. The two of them are supposed to be played together. Well, I mean one after the other, of course, but in a rather special way. First one, then the other, and then back to the first one. Like this—

(*Teacher writes on blackboard:*

Minuet 1
Minuet 2
Minuet 1)

Now what do you notice about that? Look at it.
Please, sir, it's like ABA.
Good. It's like ABA, or Ternary form. But you remember that each of the minuets was *already* in Ternary form.

(*Adds to blackboard diagram:*

Minuet 1   A :‖: B A :‖
Minuet 2   C :‖: D C :‖
Minuet 1   A ‖   B A ‖)

You'll notice I've put CDC because these are different tunes from A and B. And do you notice I've not put the repeat dots in Minuet 1 when it comes round the second time? We'll listen to the whole piece now. I want you to watch the blackboard and keep the place. Afterwards tell me which tune you like the best, A, B, C, or D.

(*Teacher plays whole movement, watching pupils' faces closely for signs of perplexity or flagging interest. If there were any he would point to the appropriate letter on the board, or call it out, or ask a particular pupil what it was.*)

Right. Did you enjoy listening to that? It's quite a good piece, when you know it. Which tune did you like the best?

(*Collection of several answers reveals C to be most liked.*)

Yes, I always like C very much. Especially when it first comes. Did you notice what a complete change it made, just when we were getting a bit tired of the first tune? That's partly because it's a new tune, of course, but also because it's in a different key. And in a different *style*—it was smooth after the rather jerky first minuet. The composer has deliberately made a contrast for the middle part of his music. Now, lots of composers did this in the eighteenth century—had two contrasting minuets and made an ABA shape out of them. In fact, they were so keen on the contrast that they gave the second minuet to only three instruments. That made it quieter, of course. Does anyone know what a piece for three instruments is called? . . . Yes, a trio. So they called the second minuet the Trio. And the funny thing is we always call it the Trio now, even when it's not composed for three instruments!

(*Rubs out 'Minuet 2' and puts 'Trio'.*)

And we say that the whole piece is in Minuet and Trio form—*not* in Ternary form. So you have just heard the Minuet and Trio from—what was it?

(*Hands are raised.*)

Yes, the 'Haffner' Symphony, by Mozart. (*Pretending surprise.*) Why, I left the word 'Haffner' on the board! Right. Now I'd like you to put a few words in your notebooks. Get ready.

(*Teacher dictates the following:*)

Minuet and Trio form

In the eighteenth century minuets were often found in pairs. The second minuet was at first played by three instruments, so as to make a contrast; therefore it was called the Trio. After the Trio the first minuet was played again without repeats. Note: each minuet was usually in Ternary form.

Minuet	A :‖: B A :‖
Trio	C :‖: D C :‖
Minuet	A ‖ B A ‖

Right. Before we go there's time for another piece. This is another Minuet and Trio by Mozart, a very good piece. The main part is vigorous and jolly and the Trio is more soothing. Don't bother to analyse this. Just enjoy it.

(*Record of Minuet and Trio from Eine Kleine Nachtmusik*)

SUNDRY MATTERS

Something must now be said about the teacher's preparation for his lesson. Quite apart from the individual lesson, the best preparation lies in the teacher's soaking himself in music and musical knowledge of all kinds. He must be a constant listener to broadcasts, records, and live concerts; a constant performer; and a constant reader of books, articles, and not least scores. This general preparation (which goes on all the teacher's lifetime) makes him a balanced person musically, and better and better able to understand and explain single pieces of music. As to the preparation of individual pieces, it goes without saying that no sane teacher will attempt to use a piece he has not thoroughly studied beforehand, at least from the particular angle he intends to show in the lesson. (A possible exception may be an experimental desire to discover the music along with his pupils.) Piano pieces should present little difficulty, but orchestral records need much listening (preferably with score) before the teacher knows his way about the music. For this reason the beginner may be better off using a record he is really familiar with, even if it is not absolutely ideal for its purpose. It is quite often appropriate for the teacher to drop a short remark or two whilst the music is playing: perhaps when illustrating a Form lesson he will point out the various sections a second before they are reached in the music, or in the case of such pieces as *The Sorcerer's Apprentice* or *Till Eulenspiegel* the various events are best described (briefly) during the music if the pupil is to associate the correct section of the music with a particular happening. All this obviously calls for intimate knowledge on the teacher's part. Wherever possible the teacher should be able to play themes, etc., on the piano *from memory*. Though this is not essential, it does away with fumbling with pages and losing time, and —even more important—atmosphere, when he is putting over an explanation or analysis.

Talking about atmosphere leads us to the use of the gramophone. Clumsiness in putting on records and handling the instrument can spoil atmosphere quite easily. Record-players differ so much that I can lay down few rules about their use, but I can plead that the teacher familiarises himself *perfectly* with the workings of his own instrument. (Dare I breathe that I have generally found women the worst offenders here? They often seem unable to cope with the simplest mechanisms and are very apt to scratch records with the stylus.) It is often necessary to play only a part of a record. To avoid ugly sounds and possible damage when beginning in the middle of a disc, use the following procedure. With turntable at rest and volume at nil, carefully lower the pickup arm on to the disc a fraction before the estimated place. Set the turntable going and raise the volume very slightly so that only the teacher hears it. When the correct place is reached increase the volume to normal. To stop in the middle, first lower the volume to nil, then stop the turntable and finally lift off the pickup arm. If, however, the machine is of the type in which the pickup arm operates the turntable motor, then lowering and raising the arm will have to be done with the turntable in motion. This calls for great care to avoid damaging the record. However, the volume should still be turned right down whenever the arm is raised or lowered. Another reason for lowering the volume is to make comments without stopping the music: here the volume is lowered only sufficient for the teacher's voice to be heard clearly. One, of course, weighs the pros and cons—the commentary has to be of more value to the pupils (on this occasion) than the passage supplanted. All these procedures again underline the importance of knowing the record well.

If a good tape-recorder is available, the teacher has a potential aid in presenting his lessons. But it must give first-class reproduction: this is normally possible only if there is some means of coupling the instrument to a large loudspeaker. Given this, and a direct-wire connexion to the record-player when recording (do *not* use the microphone), extracts from records can be presented in a prearranged order without the slightest fumbling, merely by starting and stopping the tape when giving the lesson. The technique is to wire up a direct line from the record-player (from the extension speaker socket if it possesses one) *without* disconnecting the main speaker of the record-player. This is most important. Have the tape-recorder switched to 'Record', but not running, and its volume to nil. Play the record until a couple of seconds before the wanted passage, start the tape-recorder and then turn up the volume very swiftly at the exact moment the passage is reached. At the conclusion of the extract, quickly fade out the tape-recorder volume control and then stop the tape running. If an 'artistic' fade-up and fade-out are required, then the volume control can be turned more slowly. However, one thing must be made quite clear: it is against the law to make such recordings from commercially produced records without first writing to the record company involved and seeking permission to do so. This will normally be granted when the tape is to be used for educational purposes. The teacher must make up his mind whether it is worth all the trouble, or whether he would rather fumble about on the disc or play his illustrations on the piano. Thus in the specimen lesson I have given above, wherever a section of the music (such as an 8-bar sentence) is played, this could be done by means of whichever method the teacher prefers. The slick and sure results which a made-up tape gives have to be weighed against the trouble involved in writing to the record companies, to say nothing of the time and trouble taken in making the recording in its correct sequence. No doubt the best solution is to use tape only for difficult and complicated illustrations, or those in which is it considered important to have the orchestral sound (or whatever it is) of the recording rather than its equivalent on the piano. Perhaps also a tape is useful for a lesson involving short extracts from many different pieces: here the saving of time (in the lesson!) is considerable.

Another matter which may perplex the beginner is the proportion of time which should be spent on talk, etc., compared with that spent on playing and listening to music. Without wishing to lay down any rule for this, I would suggest that the sound of music itself should occupy roughly half a lesson, and the rest of the lesson be spent talking or writing. Most of this talking will be done by the teacher, normally. But all depends how the lesson is going. A long piece of music may have to be interrupted if the class gets restive; a discussion may be prolonged if it is really leading somewhere, and so on.

MEETING THE PUPIL HALF-WAY

In general, if a class does not like the music presented by its teacher, the latter is failing in his job. After all, what he is trying to do is to teach his charges to appreciate music. Naturally to achieve this with *all* of them, *all* of the time, is impossible and no one expects it. So we don't worry overmuch about the odd one or two pupils who show dislike for this or that piece. But what about the occasional truculent individual who makes a point of airing publicly his opposition to your music? The best treatment is *not* to tell him he's wrong, but to make it clear that he has a right to his opinion, but no right to express it unless it is based on facts. Does he *understand* the music? If he doesn't, this explains his dislike. His best plan is to listen again and try harder. But let's have no mistake—if he does understand the music and can back up his dislike with facts, his views are worth listening to. In any case the teacher should

try to keep track of his pupils' musical tastes and do
some hard thinking if matters like this keep going badly
wrong.

One good way to keep track is to have an end-of-term
request session of records from the school stock, or even a
free-for-all when children may bring their own discs. In
the latter case it will be an unusually lucky teacher who
doesn't get a shower of unworthy rubbish brought to
school. But play fair and let them have their pound of
flesh. The 'pop' disease is so widespread these days that no
child seems to escape it. In most cases this doesn't seem to
prevent a love of good music from co-existence. If the
teacher can even be knowledgeable about the 'groups', he
will command respect. To show disgust at the sounds of
these records (and they are mostly undeniably disgusting)
will achieve little. Better to keep a calm face and insist on
your pound of flesh. It is, after all, a music period and not
Housewives' Choice, so the pieces should be listened to
with proper attention and treated like any other piece—
analysed and discussed if necessary. If this is done every
term, it shouldn't be long before a few good records
appear. Rejoice if they do: after all, most homes possess
only a rash of cheap seven-inch pop discs; one can't really
expect classical L.P.s to come crowding in on all sides. If
you would really rather avoid the 'pop' question, it is
better not to invite the pupils' records at all. But sooner or
later the question is bound to come up, so have an attitude
ready. One good defence is to say to the pupil who asks
for 'pop': 'What has it to do with a music lesson? Do you
ask your English teacher for Superman comics? Do you
expect to play marbles in P.E. lessons? You can have all
these things, if you want them, in your own spare time—
you don't need a teacher to help you.' But try not to put

it as succinctly as the teacher who said : 'You come here to learn, not to enjoy yourself.'

Some teachers might feel that jazz is a subject worth taking a little more seriously (I'm one, for instance.) There are many intriguing things that could be taught about its methods of performance and history. But don't attempt it without some genuine personal enthusiasm (to say nothing of some genuine personal records!).

Finally a word about humour. It is not out of place in *any* subject taught in school. There is always a danger that music might be treated too solemnly, so please don't forget to smile and crack a joke whenever possible. It may not always be easy—whenever I'm desperate I tell the one about the triangle player with 100 bars rest who managed to slip out for a drink . . . but I expect you've heard it.

8. The Philosophy of Music

INTRODUCTION

In Chapter 1 I suggested that the teacher should regard himself in the nature of an interpreter: that is, by virtue of his knowledge of music he directs his pupils' attention to the most important aspects of a piece of music, or offers them an interpretation which he considers a true one. During the rest of the book I have outlined various methods of approaching music, and of presenting it to a class. I feel I cannot leave the reader without stimulating him to think out a little further the true nature of what he is interpreting, in the hope that he will interpret better. What follows is a theoretical explanation of the listening process—a hypothesis, if you will, which I have arrived at over the course of many years—and it is presented so that the reader may ponder it and think the matter further for himself. It is necessarily given in a brief form, for this is not the place for a closely argued exposition of my theories —this would need a book to itself—and it is not vital that the reader should agree with my attitude, so long as the process of disagreement causes him to clarify his own attitude to the subject.

THE NATURE OF THE MUSICAL EXPERIENCE

I believe that the normal or 'best' musical experience, whilst somewhat complex, is basically a feeling of pleasure.

This pleasure is made up of four contributory factors:

(1) Sensuous pleasure
(2) Kinaesthetic pleasure
(3) Intellectual pleasure
(4) Aesthetic pleasure

Let me first define these terms, adding a few remarks by way of amplification.

SENSUOUS PLEASURE

I take it that all music-lovers like to some extent the sheer sound of music, that is, a single violin note will give a simple pleasure that may be described as sensuous. Some sounds may seem more pleasant than others: perhaps a celesta or vibraphone may please more than a violin. Again we may *dislike* certain sounds: I have never been able to listen willingly to electric guitars; others I know cannot bear the sound of the organ or even the violin; yet others cannot stand high notes of any kind. These dislikes may arise for some physical reason connected with the hearing process. However, assuming the normal person's tolerance of, or liking for, the ordinary sound of music, we may say that this sensuous pleasure is part of his total enjoyment. It goes farther than single notes. Surely the normal music-lover gets pleasure from hearing a simple chord or chordal progression, or even from a complete musical style. The absence of sensuous pleasure can be a serious bar to the enjoyment of music. Think for example of the throaty singer who puts you off even thinking about the music— you just wish he would go away. On the other hand, you may enjoy the sound of a fine singer's voice so much you don't care what he sings so long as you can listen.

KINAESTHETIC PLEASURE

This means quite simply our physical response to the rhythm of the music. In other words we tap our feet, nod our heads, snap our fingers, etc., or we even get up and dance. Whatever operation we allow our bodies to perform in response to the sounds of music, it will be rhythmically regular: it will conform to a regular pulse. Notice that the complexities of modern rhythm confuse the listener and *inhibit* his motor response (one reason why so many people dislike modern music!). So to some extent does classical music in which the beats are often implied and have to be supplied by the listener, who may well give up the struggle and declare that the music has no beat. (One reason for Bach's popularity is doubtless the continual obviousness of the beat in his music.) The importance of the kinaesthetic response to music must on no account be underrated. Without it a large part of music would be meaningless. It has an importance reaching far beyond its obvious manifestations.

INTELLECTUAL PLEASURE

Let there be no confusion about the word intellectual. By it I imply, not the upper-crust, culture-loving, 'superior' or 'clever' activities of man, but anything involving thinking in the three main aspects of perceiving, remembering, and reasoning. Thus the immediate repetition of a phrase or theme depends on the intellect of the listener for its appreciation. The fact that this may be done on an elementary, even crude, level does not detract from the point in the least. It is the mind of the listener that must deal with this sort of phenomenon. On the ability of the listener to perceive, remember, recognise, and compare obviously depend all the principles of musical form. The point of a recapitulation is lost unless it is recognised. The point of a variation is lost unless the listener knows both that it is the same as the original and that it is in some way different. Textural devices such as canon, imitation, and fugue depend entirely on recognition and comparison. So do inversion and augmentation. (The usual objection to the device of cancrizans, or playing a theme backwards, is that in most cases this device cannot be recognised as such and is therefore useless.) At every turn the co-operation of the mind is invited. More subtle refinements appear, such as the creation of an expectation and a thwarting of its fulfilment, ambiguities, allusions to other styles, and quotations from other works. Any kind of musical analysis involves the listener in intellectual activity—he looks at the various parts and attempts to discover the nature of their relationships with each other. There can be little doubt that the intellectual side of listening to music is both important and neglected or misunderstood. This is the aspect of listening which most needs teaching, and yet teaching of it is often resisted violently by some people. They protest that analysis is cold and that it will destroy beauty. One finds this attitude in both children and adults (expressed in different ways, no doubt). I have certainly run across my share of doubters, whose plausible moan 'But this sort of thing takes all the pleasure out of music' is not easy to refute with an epigrammatic reply. One knows that such people are wrong (in fact, are probably mentally lazy), and that intellectual effort, whilst it may cause us to lose sight of beauty temporarily, does in the end *increase* one's pleasure. One knows that composers did not put various devices and relationships into their music in order that they might go unnoticed. But it is difficult to convince these people on the spot. One has to ask them to give our system a trial and trust the music not to wither away (it is, in fact, a test of good music that it stands up to analysis). Certainly many of the wonders to be found in compositions of genius lie on the intellectual side. And however well equipped a composer may be to express himself emotionally, he is not thought highly of unless he can order his work intellectually.

Now, what is the nature of the listener's intellectual response? Chiefly it consists of *understanding*. There is a pleasure in understanding things. It is a difficult pleasure to explain, but it is almost universally felt. It is the joy of mastering a difficulty, and it has its roots in the instincts of curiosity and acquisitiveness. It may even vicariously supply a feeling of creativeness. It includes admiration for the real creator of whatever is understood, especially where this is a work of art.

AESTHETIC PLEASURE

This is our response to the perception of beauty. The concept of beauty is a complex one, and difficult or impossible to define. However, instances of beauty are recognisable to all of us. We don't all agree precisely which pieces are, or are not, beautiful; but the facts suggest that there is a strong measure of agreement among experts— in other words, trained perception would seem to discover beauty with something like reliability. Argument about what precise quality in an object constitutes beauty is, and always has been, fruitless. It is also fruitless in the last and nearly every other resort to expect others to share one's idea of beauty, or to hold up an example of the beautiful and expect others automatically to appreciate it. The task of the teacher of Musical Appreciation includes,

certainly, the constant holding up of good examples in the
hope that others may catch, as it were, the infection of their
beauty; but there is no way to *teach* what beauty is. We
have to lead horses to water and hope that they will drink.

Yet I must emphasise that an enormous part of one's
emotional response to music is due to a recognition of
beauty. We constantly find beauties in music and marvel
at them. They fill us with the strong emotional force of
admiration of beauty. This latter comes nearest to the emotion
of joy, though it is deeper and richer, and may at times
move one to tears. And let us not be misled by the tears:
they are very often *not* concerned with 'sad' music, but
are the result of a sudden deep affection for the beauty of
the music, which may be joyful or tranquil in mood.

EMOTION IN MUSIC

Before going on to describe the relationship between the
above four pleasures, I must turn attention to the question
of emotion in music. Most people agree that music pro-
duces emotions, or expresses emotions, or is concerned with
emotions in some way. Indeed, Deryck Cooke in *The
Language of Music* goes so far as to show that music is the
language of the emotions; that emotion, in fact, is what
music is all about. It is here that I venture upon my most
controversial assertion: I wish to suggest that *the conveying
of emotion through music is unimportant and incidental in the
same sense that the conveying of a 'programme' is unimportant
and incidental*. Space does not permit me here to prove this
at length, but I will urge the reader to consider the following points:

(1) Most of the emotions such as fear, anxiety, envy,
love, etc., can only be vaguely hinted at through associa-
tion of ideas (just as a 'programme' is). This is why a group

of listeners will differ in their interpretations—they each have a different set of mental associations according to temperament and musical upbringing.

(2) The emotions most easily expressed are joy and sorrow. Indeed, Cooke's list of sixteen basic musical formulae have meanings (according to him) which easily reduce to these two. Of what use would it be to devote the entire art of music to expressing these two ideas? Granted, there are finer shades of meaning within the two categories, but this would still not explain why for centuries millions of people have been concerned to express and understand such simple things so many times over, if indeed music were mainly the art of conveying emotions.

(3) We certainly respond by having feelings when we hear music. But this is mainly the fourfold pleasure described above. When we simultaneously (*a*) feel this pleasure, (*b*) *recognise* an emotional allusion in the music; we may all too easily mistake one for the other and believe the emotion to be real. No doubt it *is* more real for some listeners than others: according to one's psychological make-up one allows oneself to be more, or less, persuaded by this illusion.

(4) A test of the above statement may be made by selecting a piece of music which, in your opinion, is a thoroughly bad piece and yet which is supposed to be emotional (some fourth-rate nineteenth-century romantic piece, maybe, or a modern popular ballad). Does this make you feel? Again, can you not think of examples of fine music which you admire, and yet which, if you are honest, do not express any particular emotion? (Be careful not to count a piece as the expression of joy simply because of the fourfold pleasure you feel.)

(5) If the emotion conveyed in the music were really

felt by the listener, why should anyone listen to sad music? Again the answer must be that the fourfold pleasure far outweighs the 'sadness'.

FINAL CONSIDERATIONS

The ideal musical experience, then, is a compound of sensuous, kinaesthetic, intellectual, and aesthetic pleasures; together with a due recognition of any emotional or programmatic allusions the music may yield. The proportional importance of each factor does, of course, vary from one piece to another (and, regrettably, from one listener to another): but I will go so far as to say that on the whole the aesthetic experience is the biggest contribution, followed by the intellectual. The process of bringing people to love and understand music consists of an attempt to achieve the correct harmonious proportions between the various factors.

Let us realise that one enormous bar to the understanding of music is the fact that perception is very seldom complete enough to put the listener in possession of all the facts he needs to achieve this harmonious result. On the 'vertical' plane, he may hear clearly only the surface melody and find all lower pitches a muddy cloud in which he can distinguish little or no detail. On the 'horizontal' plane, he may have patches of mind-wandering; so that, whether or not he previously heard the surface melody only or everything, his attention 'collapses' and has to recuperate before getting back to the matter in hand. *The teacher's biggest task is to secure as complete a percepion as possible in his pupils*.

The teacher's task also includes an attempt to increase the fourfold pleasure. Teaching perception is half the battle, but it is worth while taking a final look at what else the teacher may profitably do. To increase three of the pleasures there is little that can be done except bring the pupil into contact with much music. But the increase of the intellectual pleasure is the most easily brought about. It will by now be apparent that I believe the exercise of the intellect to be important above all, for it spreads its benign influence over all the things that matter in music. The appreciation of beauty, though unteachable direct, comes through the grasping, by the mind, of relationships. The art of the composer lies in relationships—relationships of all kinds—one note to another, one instrument to another, one chord to another, one theme to another, one movement to another. They cannot be fully grasped without analysis, or repeated hearings, or both. Thus the student who approaches music in order to discover details is rewarded by the discovery of beauty—the source of the real emotional life of the music-lover. And beauty in music must exist in music's own terms, not as a representation of pictorial or literary ideas, nor as expression of a composer's emotions, nor even as the embodiment of a philosophy. The message of music is ultimately not 'Isn't life wonderful?' (or miserable, or whatever mood the composer may be thought to be expressing) but 'Look at this beauty'. Those who see the beauty will find it to be purely musical and abstract.

And so the 'interpretation' referred to in Chapter 1 which the teacher passes on to his pupils is not so much a description of emotions; still less is it a cataloguing of imaginative fantasies: it is the careful drawing of the pupils' attention to whatever in the teacher's opinion matters most about a piece of music. It is the teacher's personal way of showing where beauty may be found. This, then, is the way to teach Musical Appreciation.

Suggestions for Further Reading

Antony Baines: *Musical Instruments through the Ages* (Penguin).
A very useful handbook packed with information.
Deryck Cooke: *The Language of Music* (O.U.P.).
This is particularly relevant to the general discussion in Chapters 1 and 8.
Cedric Thorpe Davie: *Musical Structure and Design* (Dobson).
The best available book on Musical Form.
Alfred Einstein: *A Short History of Music*, illustrated edition (Cassell).
A good history, with many interesting illustrations.
Stewart Macpherson: *Form in Music* (Joseph Williams).
A good traditional account.
R. O. Morris: *The Structure of Music* (O.U.P.).
Quite short; very clear and readable.
Allen Percival: *Teach Yourself History of Music* (English Universities Press).
Rather freely, and not always accurately, written: nevertheless a stimulating and readable book. Should be used as a supplementary rather than a prime source of information.
Walter Piston: *Orchestration* (Gollancz).
One of the best of the standard textbooks. For background reading on the properties of various instruments.
Priestley & Fowler: *A Music Guide for Schools* (Nelson).
Pages 164–84 are useful on Colour.

Alec Robertson and Denis Stevens: *The Pelican History of Music* (Penguin).

Another good, reasonably short history.

Percy Scholes: *Music: the Child and the Masterpiece* (O.U.P.).

Although this is now out of print, copies should be obtainable through local libraries. It is inevitably dated in parts (it was first published in 1935), but contains a great deal of good sense and thought-provoking comment.

Donald F. Tovey: *The Forms of Music* (O.U.P.).

A collection of articles, originally published in the *Encyclopedia Britannica*, covering all the principal musical forms with Tovey's usual brilliance.

Index